D1612547

Concise guides
to planning

Planning,
Sustainability
and Nature

Planning, Sustainability and Nature

**Dave Counsell
and Rob Stoneman**

First published in 2018 by Lund Humphries

Lund Humphries
Office 3, Book House
261A City Road
London EC1V 1JX
UK
www.lundhumphries.com
Planning, Sustainability and Nature
© Dave Counsell and Rob Stoneman, 2018
All rights reserved

ISBN (hardback): 978-1-84822-285-4
ISBN (eBook PDF): 978-1-84822-286-1
ISBN (eBook ePub): 978-1-84822-300-4
ISBN (eBook ePub Mobi): 978-1-84822-301-1
Concise Guides to Planning (Print): ISSN 2516-8177
Concise Guides to Planning (Online): ISSN 2516-8185

Designed by Stefi Orazi Studio
Cover illustration by Stefi Orazi
Set in Favorit

Image credits
Airfotos. © Banks Group: 35; Airwolfhound
cc-by-sa/2.0: 70; Avon Wildlife Trust: 96; Banks
Group: 118; Martin Batt: 136; Cornwall Wildlife Trust:
104; Devon Wildlife Trust: 99 (top); Penny Dixie,
London Wildlife Trust: 36, 94 (bottom); Dave Dunlop,
Wildlife Trust for Lancashire, Manchester, and
Merseyside: 101; Institute of Estuarine and Coastal
Studies, Nick Cutts: 75 (bottom); Chris Lawrence: 47;
Billy Lindbrom cc-by-sa/2.0: 42; Steve Marsden: 65;
Chris Miller: 24; Linda Ollier cc-by-sa/2.0: 99
(bottom); Martin Pettitt, cc-by-sa/2.0: 90; Ian Pratt:
53; Joanna Richards 12; Mike Richardson: 125;
Sheffield Wildlife Trust: 87; Jonathan Stonehouse
cc-by-sa/2.0: 30; Rob Stoneman 17, 18, 51, 62, 75 (top),
80; Steve Trotter, The Wildlife Trusts: 88 (bottom);
Yorkshire Wildlife Trust 23, 54 (Jennifer Krill), 55
(Don Vine), 64, 71, 73, 73 (bottom, Jim Horsfall), 88.1
(Sophie Pinder), 89, 93 (Joanna Richards), 94 (top,
Jackie Holder), 107, 122 (Tom Marshall), 137

Contents

Foreword

It is an enormous pleasure and privilege to introduce the first book in our new series, *Concise Guides to Planning*. *Planning, Sustainability and Nature* addresses some of the most important, challenging and fast-moving policy areas in planning today. It does so in an utterly engaging and compelling way, providing a wealth of information and informative case studies which illustrate what can be done with imagination and commitment by planners and those they work with.

The book is written by two real experts in the field, bringing a wonderful mixture of academic rigour and professional expertise and insight. The result is a book which I devoured in one sitting, something I can't ever remember doing before. This is testimony to the authors themselves but also to the mission for this book series – to provide rich, well-written and approachable texts that will help professionals to extend and update their skills and introduce students to new subject areas.

Graham Haughton, Series Editor

Preface and Acknowledgements

With their specialist language, acronyms and complex relationships, the natural sciences are not widely understood by other professions and academic disciplines, yet planners need to address many aspects of the natural environment in their professional work. Any difficulties experienced are compounded by the fact the two disciplines often have their own policy agendas reporting to different governance institutions.

This book attempts to demystify the subject, making it more accessible to planners and other built environment professionals by providing a grounding in the evolving concepts associated with biodiversity and the natural environment and in the practical application of these concepts. It addresses the shifting focus of natural environment policy, from the protection of rare species and often small nature reserves to a more holistic approach based on biodiversity and whole natural systems, looking at the implications of these shifts for planning practice. As well as traditional approaches to site designation and species protection, it will explain what is meant by concepts such as natural capital, landscape-scale conservation, connectivity of ecosystems, habitat creation, rewilding, ecosystem services, multi-functionality and re-naturing cities, and will consider how they might be addressed in urban and rural planning. The principal focus of discussions about policy will be on the UK and Europe, but a broad selection of case studies will give examples of practice from other countries throughout the world.

Overall, the book will attempt to answer the following questions:

- Why should planning professionals need to think more about these issues and have a better understanding of how the focus of policy and practice on the natural environment has shifted historically?
- Why do planners need to understand the language of environmental science and what is meant by concepts such as biodiversity, natural capital and ecosystem services?
- Why is it important to plan for the natural environment at a whole landscape scale and to connect fragmented wildlife habitats?
- Why do planners need to look beyond protecting particular species and their habitats, towards rebuilding the whole natural environment?
- Why should planners help nature to recolonise towns and cities and how best can they do this?

We have received support writing this book from a number of individuals and organisations and would particularly like to thank Rachel Hackett of The Wildlife Trusts for her invaluable help with case studies and images, and the following staff at Y orkshire Wildlife Trust: Sally Henderson and her graphics team; Sara Robin, Lauren Garside and Louise Wilkinson in the planning team; Jeremy Garside at Tees Valley Wildlife Trust for assistance with the Bowesfield case study (Case Study 43); and Imogen Davenport and Simon Cripps of Dorset Wildlife Trust for providing the Frome Valley Road case study (Case Study 44).

The photographs are mainly from The Wildlife Trusts and Yorkshire Wildlife Trust image collections. Photographers are acknowledged on page 4 and we are grateful to all the photographers for the use of their images to illustrate this publication.

Introduction

This chapter explores regulatory and policy development for nature conservation in the United Kingdom and Europe. It illustrates how early UK legislation and the European Union Nature Directives focused largely on protecting rare and declining species of plants and animals and the best examples of their habitats; many of these relatively small areas. New approaches were sought which looked at conservation more holistically and at much greater spatial scales. Many of these ideas were brought to the attention of the British Government in an influential report, *Making Space for Nature: A Review of England's Wildlife Sites and Ecological Networks* (2010). They were subsequently incorporated into a White Paper on the Natural Environment and into the National Planning Policy Framework and Planning Policy Guidance. Similar themes are addressed in policy statements emerging from Europe such as the EU's Biodiversity Strategy to 2020.

Origins of nature conservation in the UK

Conserving land for nature has a long history in the UK. Wild areas of land, such as the royal forests in England, have been given a degree of protection since Norman times, though these were managed largely for the protection of game (principally deer and wild boar), not for the natural environment itself. Nevertheless, Forest Law did protect many areas of woodland and heath which might otherwise have been cultivated. The New Forest is a prime example of a royal forest whose habitat has survived to the present time and even retains the medieval court that looks after its interests: the Verderers.

The origins of the modern conservation movement can be found in the natural history societies established during the nineteenth and early twentieth centuries, for example Royal Society for the Protection of Birds (1889), National Trust (1895), Society for the Promotion of Nature Reserves (1912, now the Royal Society of Wildlife Trusts). Charles Rothschild published the first comprehensive list of potential nature reserves in the UK in 1915. Early conservation movements also arose in the United States where the focus was on the preservation of wilderness – the first national park in the world was Yellowstone in 1872, followed by Yosemite in 1890.

Parallel to movements to protect wildlife in the countryside were movements to provide accessible green areas in towns. Urban parks had been established as early as the seventeenth century (Hyde Park, 1637) but the main period of park development was in the nineteenth century, by the end of which citizens of most northern industrial towns and cities had access to parks. In the United States parks were created at a greater metropolitan scale, New York's Central Park (1857) being a prime example. The late nineteenth century also witnessed the birth of the garden city movement based on the writings of Ebenezer Howard – new self-sufficient communities living in the countryside surrounded by greenbelt and built around a central garden hub.

←
Central Park,
New York.

Development of UK nature conservation policy

During the height of the Second World War, with bombs raining over London, civil servants, experts, policy makers and academics began planning for the peace. Organised by the Society for the Promotion of Nature Reserves (now the Royal Society of Wildlife Trusts), one such grouping got together for a conference on Nature Preservation in Post-War Construction in 1941.[1] By 1942 this had morphed into a formal Government Committee: the Nature Reserves Investigation Committee, leading to a Green Paper – Command 7122 Conservation of Nature in England and Wales – that detailed how to set up a state nature conservation system in the UK.[2] Eventually, this led to the groundbreaking 1949 National Parks Act, with the Peak District becoming the UK's first national park in 1950. This Act did much more than simply set up national parks. It organised the UK's first state nature conservation service – the Nature Conservancy; it set out legislation to protect biologically rich areas as Sites of Special Scientific Interest (SSSI) to be conserved through the local planning system; and it empowered the Nature Conservancy to declare and manage National Nature Reserves and local authorities to do the same for Local Nature Reserves.

The reconstruction of post-war Britain had wildlife and landscape at its heart. Yet, despite such efforts, wildlife began to decline at an alarming rate. In part this was due to gamekeepers who shot out many predators in the countryside to protect recreational shooting. Some of this was addressed through the 1954 Wild Birds Act that made it illegal to kill or take the eggs of all birds, apart from some pest species. However, rapid development destroyed some of the best sites for wildlife (see Case Study 1) whilst the 'juggernaut' of intensive agriculture massively reduced the diversity and abundance of wildlife across the UK countryside.[3] For example, of the 182 potential nature reserves identified by Rothschild and his associates in England at the beginning of the twentieth century, 21 have now been completely destroyed and 142 partially destroyed. All but 19 have suffered little or no loss.[4]

Indeed, designation of sites under the National Parks Act as SSSIs was actually rather weak. All that was required under the legislation was for the Nature Conservancy (and its successors) to notify local planning authorities that an SSSI existed. The Nature Conservancy was given the power to enter into management agreements with landowners to maintain the interest of SSSIs with the Countryside Act of 1968 but was given little resource to enact such agreements.

Case Study 1   **Cow Green Reservoir**

Upper Teesdale is famed by botanists for its outstanding diversity of rare alpine and arctic flora – plants such as mountain avens, marsh saxifrage, hoary rock-rose and spring gentian – particularly over outcrops of sugar limestone. In 1967, when chemical company ICI applied to flood part of Upper Teesdale, conservationists were horrified and launched a massive campaign. Despite SSSI status, the campaign failed, and Cow Green Reservoir was built, but politicians were taken aback by the vehemence of the campaign and within a few years the first Ministers for the Environment were appointed. The weakness of legislation designed to protect Britain's wildlife was horribly exposed.

Legislative weakness in protecting important wildlife sites was exposed again and again. Construction of the M3, for example, had the look of an SSSI dot-to-dot map with the motorway slicing through SSSI heathlands and woodlands all along its route. Through the 1970s, non-governmental organisations (NGOs) lobbied for stronger protection, arguing for legislation to stop damaging activities on SSSIs.

This led to the Wildlife and Countryside Act (1981). With this Act, the Nature Conservancy Council (NCC) was given powers to notify all owners and occupiers of the special features of SSSIs as well as placing a requirement on SSSI managers to notify the NCC before carrying out any potentially damaging operations. At this stage, the NCC could attempt to discourage SSSI managers from damaging the site or negotiate compensatory management agreements for profits foregone as a result of not carrying out a damaging operation. The approach helped but did not stop the continued destruction of the UK's best wildlife sites.

The road-building programme during the 1980s was particularly infamous with the A34–M40 (Southampton to

Birmingham) route (see Case Study 2) leading to dramatic road protests that mired the projects in controversy and added huge extra costs. The Newbury bypass protests were particularly active, with tree houses and tunnels, making one of the protestors (Daniel Hooper, aka Swampy) so famous he appeared as a guest on *Have I Got News for You* on BBC1.

Case Study 2 **St Catherine's Hill**

Perhaps one of the worst examples of environmental damage due to road building occurred at St Catherine's Hill. Just outside Winchester, this Hampshire and Isle of Wight Wildlife Trust Nature Reserve contains unimproved chalk grassland. Chalk grasslands were once common across the chalklands of England, a grassland habitat first developed by domestic grazing in Neolithic times. These grasslands are rich in flowers supporting diverse assemblages of butterflies and moths. In the 1950s, chalk grasslands were still abundant – Lousley, for example, noted that 'the short dense turf occupied countless acres of Wiltshire, Hampshire, Berkshire and Dorset downland'.[5] However, artificial fertilisers allowed farmers to plough these grasslands, creating arable land, and only a few fragments remain, mainly on steeper slopes such as St Catherine's Hill. The Hill also contained exceptionally important archaeology – an Iron Age hill fort, barrows, burial mounds and a medieval maze. Not surprisingly, St Catherine's Hill was one of the earliest SSSIs to be designated in 1951, just two years after the 1949 National Parks Act came into force. Despite this designation and its obvious importance, the A34 was rerouted straight through the middle of the nature reserve by building a huge cutting.

Another issue is that SSSI designation was never meant to be comprehensive. The series was set up to be representative of the wildlife it sought to protect. The intention was that SSSI designation was simply one mechanism to conserve wildlife, with published guidelines noting that nature conservation was just as essential outside the network, but that non-statutory means such as advice, education and persuasion had to be used.[6] In essence, most wildlife-rich sites were not designated and had no protection.

Local Wildlife Sites offered a more formal means for providing local authorities with such advice. Groups of experts, often including local naturalist organisations, The Wildlife Trusts and local authority ecologists, formed local committees to select those sites that were important for wildlife but not (or yet to be) designated as an SSSI. Local authorities, recognising the robustness of the system, often included these sites into local plans, adding planning guidance to steer development away from these sites. Different authorities used and still use different terms – Sites of Importance to Nature Conservation (SINCs), Sites of Biological Importance (SBIs), County Wildlife Sites (CoWS). Collectively they are known as Local Wildlife Sites. In effect, these sites are afforded the same protection as SSSIs used to have prior to the 1981 Wildlife and Countryside Act – they are a non-statutory method of providing local authorities information in relation to planning development. Many local plans are explicit that development will generally be refused if it damages or destroys a Local Wildlife Site, unless there are overriding reasons (see Chapter 6).

—
International developments in nature conservation policy
Wildlife conservation was as much an international as a national affair in the post-war period, with the development of the International Union for the Protection of Nature set up as part of UNESCO in 1948. An example of such cooperation was the Ramsar Convention of 1971 which committed countries to conserving their most important wetland sites, though for the UK it was membership of the EU that had greater impact and in particular the Wild Bird Directive (1979) and the Habitats Directive (1992) implemented through the Wildlife and Countryside Act (1981) and the Habitats Regulations (1994) respectively. These Directives called on the UK to designate sites as Special Protection Areas (for birds) or Special Areas of Conservation (for habitats and other rare species) and enact strict protection measures. This was a crucial change. For the first time, important sites could not be damaged unless there was overriding national interest. As importantly, any development affecting these sites had to undergo a formal impact assessment and the Government had to ensure management to maintain or restore the

conservation interest. Britain finally had legislation that could stop damaging development, although it was not always successful in doing this (see Case Study 3 and Chapter 6).

Case Study 3   **Thorne and Hatfield Moors**

A particularly good example of the power of the Habitats Directive is Thorne and Hatfield Moors – the two largest lowland raised bogs in the UK, in South Yorkshire. Both were designated, in part, as SSSIs with part of Thorne Moor designated as a National Nature Reserve. Both sites had been exploited for peat – first for fuel, then for animal bedding – for centuries, creating a patchwork of cuttings and intact peat. Mining of peat for horticultural production ramped up destruction such that the Moors were largely devoid of vegetation by the early 1980s. Despite such extensive damage, conservationists argued that the Moors were still the largest extant lowland raised bog in England and should be declared a Special Area of Conservation (SAC) under the Habitats Directive. The Joint Nature Conservation Committee, set up after splitting the NCC into country bodies, disagreed and the first lists sent to the European Commission did not include the Moors. The environmental NGOs formally complained, compiling their own list of sites;[7] a complaint that was upheld by the Commission, forcing the JNCC to resubmit the national list. Thorne and Hatfield Moors were then designated, and the Government compensated Scotts (the peat mining company) for revocation of planning permission. Today the Moors are managed as a National Nature Reserve under restoration to raised bog in line with the Habitats Directive.

→
Restoration of Hatfield Moor. Peat mining left the surface bare of any vegetation. Low bunded cells are created that fill with rainwater, allowing vegetation to re-establish.

In the absence of pan-national political institutions such as the EU, Government policy to protect nature falls to nation states, which are strongly influenced by International Convention.

For example, in South East Asia important international policy drivers for the conservation of nature include the Convention on Biological Diversity, the Convention on Migratory Species, the Convention on Wetlands (Ramsar), the Convention on International Trade in Endangered Species of Wild Fauna and Flora and the United Nations Convention on Climate Change.[8] Trans-boundary cooperation can be important. In South East Asia, for example, burning of cleared and drained peatlands has generated extreme levels of smoke. This trans-boundary haze is estimated to have caused economic losses of over $US 16 billion in 2015.[9] As a result, the Association of South East Asian Nations has set up a trans-boundary approach to deal with the issue, requiring each nation to develop and implement its own strategies. The Reducing Emissions from Deforestation and Degradation mechanism within the Kyoto Protocol of the Climate Change Convention has a role in enabling developed countries to pay developing countries such as Indonesia to reduce emissions from peat-swamp forests in South East Asia through their conservation. At a more local level, these international policy

←
Burnt peat swamp forest in Brunei Darussalam, SE Asia.

drivers are enacted through a variety of land-use planning tools, such as designation. In Indonesia, for example, forests are protected from exploitation through designation for conservation (*Hutan konservii*) or biodiversity (*Hutan lindung*), though enforcement of such protections is often a critical failing.

Canada has a similar nested approach. International Convention is translated into Federal Policy, which in the case of Canada sets a series of objectives which the Federal Government will support, such as no net loss of wetlands. Nature conservation is then devolved to the Provinces and Territories. Here, policy can vary. For example, protection of wetlands in Alberta is much weaker than it is in Nova Scotia, though it can be argued that the threats are far lower in the sparsely inhabited north of Canada such as Alberta.

Recent policy developments

Despite the provisions of the Habitats Directive, continuing high profile cases of damage to SSSIs (see Case Study 4) continued to expose the weakness of the UK's site protection system. After a huge lobbying effort by the environmental NGOs, a new Act came into force – the Countryside and Rights of Way Act (CROW) (2000). For its New Labour architects, this was as much about opening access to commons and uplands. For Britain's beleaguered wildlife, the Act finally ensured SSSIs were protected by statute. The Act meant that any impact on an SSSI had to be permitted by the NCC and its successor bodies in England – English Nature and Natural England. Moreover, the NCC had the right to enter management agreements with owner/occupiers to manage SSSIs towards favourable conservation status. Some measure of financial ability to enter into those management agreements came through the Agenda 2000 Common Agricultural Policy (CAP) reforms in 1999 that facilitated rural development monies (so called pillar 2 of the CAP) to enable better management. If a development could not be relocated and was deemed of national significance, then the impact had to be fully mitigated (often through habitat creation close to the SSSI).

Offham Down

In the run-up to the 1997 General Election, Offham Down, Sussex, became the poster boy for momentum towards the CROW Act (2000). Here, as in many parts of the country, a farmer had decided to plough up a chalk downland SSSI to grow flax, which at the time attracted a high agricultural subsidy payment through the CAP. Conservationists organised an extremely well-publicised army of volunteers to put back the ploughed turves of ancient chalk grassland, with Labour politicians lining up to help. In the end, the farmer was compensated, the grassland restored and nature conservation legislation firmly placed within the New Labour manifesto.

The CROW Act finally secured protection for SSSIs in England and Wales, with Scotland (2004) and Northern Ireland (2002) bringing in similar legislation slightly later. Yet, despite the provisions of the CROW Act that largely stopped destruction of SSSIs, wildlife across the UK continued its decline.

Policy development continued for England and Wales through the Natural Environment and Rural Communities (NERC) Act in 2006 that bolstered the Wildlife and Countryside Act 1981 and CROW Act. The new Act was designed to help to achieve a rich and diverse natural environment and thriving rural communities and simplified arrangements for the delivery of Government Policy. Much of this Act concerned administrative provisions, such as merging the Rural Development Service, the Countryside Agency and English Nature into a single body – Natural England. The Act clarified protected habitats and species, specifying 56 habitats and 943 species. Perhaps more importantly, the Act placed a duty to conserve biodiversity on all public authorities and statutory undertakers in England. This is important. Internal Drainage Boards, for example, were set up to provide a collective mechanism to drain farmland which can be damaging to wildlife. After the passing of the NERC Act, many Internal Drainage Boards developed Biodiversity Action Plans (BAPs) that helped them to continue drainage activities but in a way that maintained wildlife populations. Similar duties were developed in Wales, through the Environment Act Wales 2016 and in Scotland through the Wildlife and Natural Environment Scotland Act 2011.

Despite such legislative provisions, the State of Nature reports, first published in 2013 and then in 2016, showed that between 1970 and 2013, 56% of species declined, with 40% showing strong or moderate declines set against 44% of species that increased, with 29% showing strong or moderate increases.[10]

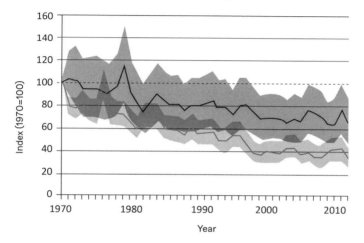

Graph showing the decline of priority species in the UK. The lower grey line is an abundance indicator for 213 priority species whilst the upper grey line is an occupancy index for 111 species. Shaded areas represent 95% confidence intervals. It is clear that, from the 1970 baseline, species have generally fared badly in the UK. Graph redrawn from the *State of Nature* 2016 report.

In 2009, the Government asked Professor Sir John Lawton to form a committee to examine whether the protected area network was adequate. They concluded:

unequivocally that it is not, and that at the present time there are real problems with the size, management and protection of our wildlife sites, linked to a range of other pressures on them. Despite our best efforts, we continue to lose species and habitats at an alarming rate. This is not to say that the current series of protected areas is of no value. Far from it. Without it the scale of losses would have undoubtedly been much worse.[11]

The authors made a strong case for *bigger* protected areas, more of them, that are better managed and, crucially, better *connected* through ecological corridors and stepping stone sites. The 'bigger, better, more and connected' mantra from the Lawton committee paralleled thinking by the major NGOs and Natural England for a well-connected ecological network of sites that could cope with shifting populations of species consequent on climate change. These were variously called Living Landscapes[12] (The Wildlife Trusts), Futurescapes[13] (RSPB) and ecological networks[14] (Natural England) but amounted to the same thing – landscape-scale restoration of wildlife.

Lawton called for large-scale ecological restoration zones. The Government responded with a White Paper published in 2011.[15] This report represents something of a watershed in Government policy for the natural environment. Here the previous emphasis on site, habitat or species protection is replaced with a much more holistic vision. The Lawton agenda is specifically picked up, with Government committing to the development of an ecological network. The first phase would be a competition to develop 12 Nature Improvement Areas (NIAs) (see Case Study 5). Over 70 applications for funding were received, demonstrating huge appetite for this approach. The Government promised to put nature into the heart of decision-making, reforming planning law for example, and also undertook to establish Local Nature Partnerships that would work alongside Local Enterprise Partnerships in developing the natural, social and economic capital. Another notable change in approach is the adoption of natural capital concepts, in which the language of economics is used to help value ecosystem services (see Chapter 2). The Government established an independent body – the Natural Capital Committee.

Unfortunately, much of the commitment in the White Paper was undone by the politics of the post 2009 economic collapse and a desire by Government to substantially reduce its spending. Natural England was slashed in size by a third whilst Local Nature Partnerships were set up without any funding; the White Paper had a limited effect.

Case Study 5   **Humberhead Levels**

The Humberhead Levels NIA spanned the former Glacial Lake
Humber area, centred on the now partially restored Thorne and
Hatfield Moors (see Case Study 3). The project, run under the
aegis of the Humberhead Levels Partnership, included a wide
group of government agencies, NGOs, internal drainage boards
and local farmers. Some 1,190ha of habitat was created,
restored and extended as part of a wider programme to restore
mainly wetland wildlife in an integrated network of sites across
what remains an intensively arable landscape.[16] The NIA project
itself, though large-scale, would not bring about an ecological
network across the Levels but is nested in a range of other
projects that, in time, could see wetland wildlife return to much
of the area.

Legend

— Rivers
---- Ditches and drains
▓ Existing natural assets
▓ Bare ground
▓ Built-up areas
░ Arable land

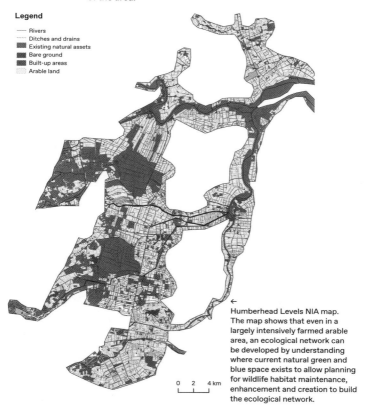

←
Humberhead Levels NIA map.
The map shows that even in a
largely intensively farmed arable
area, an ecological network can
be developed by understanding
where current natural green and
blue space exists to allow planning
for wildlife habitat maintenance,
enhancement and creation to build
the ecological network.

0   2   4 km

Linked to the Government's 2011 White Paper was planning reform. The Coalition Government had promised a 'bonfire of red-tape'.[17] Planning guidance stretched to 25 guidance notes issued over many years. Instead of this somewhat confusing and occasionally contradictory mass of guidance, a new National Planning Policy Framework (NPPF) document was devised, accompanied later by online guidance notes. Its first iteration actually weakened protection to wildlife and the environment but after a strong public campaign, led by the National Trust, the NPPF was revised with some welcome new policy to protect nature (see Case Study 6).

Case Study 6 **The Chat Moss Inquiry**

An early test of the efficacy of the new NPPF came at a Public Inquiry for an application to extend planning permission to mine peat at Chat Moss, in Salford and Wigan.

Chat Moss had once been a wide expanse of raised bog between Manchester and Liverpool. Britain's first commercial railway was actually floated on birch faggots across the moss in the early nineteenth century. Land drainage, agricultural reclamation and peat-cutting has reduced the mosslands to a few fragments that are now gradually being restored as part of the Manchester Mosslands NIA. This programme seeks to restore wetlands and other semi-natural habitats across what is

↓
Chat Moss, Greater Manchester.

now a rather messy urban fringe landscape, improving the quality of life for local residents and restoring the wetland wildlife of this once iconic peatland area.

At Chat Moss, Sinclair PLC argued that effective restoration of the peatland could only be secured through new planning permission for further peat extraction. Wigan and Salford councils disagreed, refusing planning permission on the basis that the original planning permission had already made provision for restoration and, crucially, the NPPF made it clear that new permissions for peat extraction should not be given. The Planning Inspector agreed. Five years later, the site remains only partly restored.

The Government White Paper of 2011 was clearly well intended but, with the notable exception of the 12 NIAs, lacked concrete measures to arrest the decline of wildlife in the UK. At the heart of this decline are systemic issues of climate change, atmospheric nitrogen pollution causing eutrophication (nutrient enrichment of soils), agricultural intensification, resource depletion (especially at sea), poor development and, above all else, ecological fragmentation making it more difficult to cope with these systemic issues. The White Paper offered little to address these issues and was accompanied by a public austerity programme that substantially reduced the capacity of state nature conservation to operate effectively. Local Wildlife Site systems, for example, are now compromised as fewer local authorities employ dedicated ecologists.

—

Conclusions

Ultimately, the aspirations of the 1949 National Parks Act, and the committees for nature conservation that preceded it, were not met. Very few conservationists or ecologists at the time foretold the impact of intensive agriculture that has wreaked such enormous damage to Britain's countryside. The protected area network proved entirely inadequate in the face of such massive and systemic land-use change. Indeed, perhaps it was because Britain adopted an approach that rested mainly on protected areas (and conservationists largely followed suit) that it ignored the damage to the wider environment for far too long.

The UK is now one of the most depleted nations on Earth in terms of biodiversity. The current Government has published a 25-year plan for the environment in which it sets out an approach that aims to 'leave our environment in a better state than we found it'.[18] Leaving the EU and particularly reformation of agricultural policy and fiscal mechanisms offer a huge opportunity for the UK to address some of the systemic issues affecting Britain's wildlife (see Chapter 7). Even if such opportunities are taken, restoration of wildlife in the lowlands is a substantial task requiring fundamental changes of approach, not least by development planners. Most lowland counties have lost one or more plant species each year since the war [19] and conservationists now argue for new legislation, modelled on climate change legislation, to provide statutory underpinning for a restoration of wildlife. The uplands, dominated by EU-subsidised marginal though occasionally high nature value farming, could be restored far quicker. Indeed, subsidy removal and consequent abandonment of uneconomic sheep farming in the uplands and on the marginal soils of the UK might have the unintended consequence of ecological restoration through rewilding.

—

Introduction

Chapter 2 explores the emergence of sustainable development as a policy objective of planning systems and how ideas associated with environmental sustainability such as carrying capacity, natural capital and ecosystem services became part of the rhetoric of planning policy.

Concerns about the impact of rapid population growth and the rates at which natural resources were being depleted led to a series of international conventions looking at environment and development during the later decades of the twentieth century. Perhaps the most influential of these was the report *Our Common Future*, published by the World Commission on Environment and Development in 1989. This report promoted the concept of sustainable development, which it described as: 'development that meets the needs of the present without compromising the ability of future generations to meet their own needs'.[20] This definition was perhaps intentionally vague in an attempt to achieve widespread international acceptance. However, it is hardly a blueprint for action, and has been reinterpreted many times since. It can be described as development that uses resources more efficiently than in the past, enhances, or at least does not damage the environment, and is socially equitable whilst also supporting economic development (but not necessarily economic growth). The UN Conference on Environment and Development held in Rio in 1992 (often called the Earth Summit), which called for a shift from talk to action, stimulated a renewed focus on sustainable development in public policy. In the UK, for example, the

Government produced a strategy for sustainable development[21] and a BAP [22] in the years following Rio. Planning was identified as a key area of policy to deliver sustainable development and there was much debate about how to make the concept operational.

There were many, sometimes contradictory, approaches to achieving sustainable development and not a great deal of consensus about how to deliver it. Discourses on sustainable development tended to categorise approaches as ranging from weak (light green) to strong (dark green). The strong approaches were typically grouped together under the label environmental sustainability, with characteristic rhetoric about operating within limits imposed by natural systems, thresholds beyond which development would result in catastrophic breakdown of these systems, and the necessity of maintaining levels of natural capital in the face of development pressures and resource exploitation. Attempts to deliver environmental sustainability through planning led to much speculation about whether concepts of carrying capacity, alternatively referred to as environmental capacity, and natural capital could be adapted to provide a rationale for determining how much development could be accommodated in development plans. The application of these ideas in planning practice was tested in the round of new strategic plans prepared during the later years of the twentieth century and the first decade of the twenty-first in county structure plans and regional spatial strategies in England.

Carrying capacity

Natural resource systems can be described as having environmental limits, the point or range of conditions beyond which the benefits derived from the resource system are judged unacceptable or insufficient. Environmental thresholds mark the boundary between these states. For example, a grassland habitat might provide sufficient food for a specific number of grazing animals. If that number is exceeded, the grassland suffers from overgrazing resulting in an impoverished habitat which supports fewer animals – its environmental capacity has been exceeded. Whilst this is a recognised characteristic of natural resource management, planners sought to use the same ideas to calculate how much development could be accommodated before local environments were irreparably damaged. In effect, they were attempting to use a principle of environmental sustainability as a practical tool to help them decide how much housing and economic development could be allocated in a development plan. This was controversial and strongly opposed by the development industry. A quote from a study commissioned by housing developers gives a flavour of how concerned the development industry was about the concept of carrying capacity.

> My contention is that capacity is not easily tied down and has real dangers. It is not simply that environmental capacity arguments can become a cloak for NIMBYism (and thus lose credibility). It is that in some situations the notion of capacity is just not valid.[23]

A more comprehensive attempt to explore the constraints imposed by the environment on development was that undertaken by West Sussex County Council, in preparing its structure plan. It mapped 58 environmental characteristics that would constrain development and concluded that the environment in West Sussex, and particularly the countryside environment, was deteriorating rapidly to the extent that levels of housing growth in regional guidance for the county would be unsustainable. This decision was eventually challenged by central government, which directed the county council to increase its housing numbers into line with national guidance.

Ultimately, these early experiments with carrying capacity as a planning tool failed. Environmental economist Michael Jacobs argued that environmental capacity studies provide a framework within which to make development decisions rather than providing a rigid set of constraints which could provide a technical answer to the quantity of development to be planned for. He noted: 'Capacity is a political metaphor. Environmental capacity limits are not (simply) properties of nature; they are products of social judgement about acceptable and unacceptable change.'[24]

Although experimentation with environmental capacity declined following the debates in the late 1990s, there has been some resurgence of interest. Cannock Chase District Council (Staffordshire) commissioned a study of its environmental capacity in 2013 (see Case Study 7).[25] The study acknowledged that although aspects of environmental capacity require value judgements, it did nevertheless provide a range of technical and qualitative data, which in turn provides a useful evidence base for a strategic plan. This approach was somewhat different to earlier applications of the concept and appears to take account of previous criticism of these approaches.

Case Study 7   **Cannock Chase environmental capacity study**

Concerned about the possible impact of development on the attractive environment of Cannock Chase, the district council commissioned an environmental capacity study, undertaken by Land Use Consultants. A housing market assessment had identified a need for 250 houses per annum in the district and several locations had been identified where long-term growth pressures were likely to arise. The capacity of local environments to accommodate growth were assessed against a range of constraints including air quality, water quality, water supply, flood risk, biodiversity, landscape, open space, soils, historic environment and minerals. Climate change was included as a cross-cutting constraint. Whilst much of the analysis was qualitative, it sought to be as objective as possible using accepted targets and standards where these were available.

→
Cannock Chase,
Staffordshire.

The overall level of growth and possible locations for new development were assessed against these constraints and locations colour coded to indicate whether environmental capacity would be breached. The assessment concluded that the annual level of growth proposed could probably be accommodated and the impacts mitigated, but none of the long-term locations were without potential capacity issues. One location in particular was identified as giving rise to more issues than the others. On a more general note the study commented that:

> the concept of environmental capacity is not just a technical matter. Many aspects of environmental capacity are about value judgements and particular views will depend on the circumstances of the individual or organisations involved. Environmental campaigners are more likely to consider the environmental capacity of a location being breached by a development than those more concerned with promoting economic growth.[26]

Natural capital

Natural capital, the stock of our physical natural assets such as air, water, soils, landscape and biodiversity, is another concept experimented with in development planning in the period following the 1992 Rio Earth Summit. Early attempts to incorporate the idea into planning decisions focused on distinguishing between critical natural capital, i.e. that which should be inviolable in the face of development pressures, and constant assets, i.e. capital which should be maintained at present levels and should be compensated for when lost to development. The UK Government's NCC funded research projects aimed at identifying critical natural capital in the terrestrial and marine environments. Opinions about which sorts of natural capital should be defined as critical were debated during the preparation of strategic plans and, as with environmental capacity, the West Sussex plan was again a leading proponent of this concept, arguing that strategic gaps between built-up areas should be included as critical capital. This was controversial because the strategic gaps might have in themselves little intrinsic value, *cf.* arguments often applied to greenbelt planning constraints. Jacobs commented that decisions on what types of natural capital should be inviolable in the face of development pressures will depend on human judgement and are essentially political;[27] this was undoubtedly the case in West Sussex. Others engaged in the debate took a different view, arguing that there is a continuum between critical or constant capital giving rise to inconsistent and politically driven assessment.

The expert panel which examined West Sussex County Council's structure plan concluded that 'if thresholds have to be crossed to accommodate housing and employment growth, the strategic gaps could be considered less precious than other landscape constraints'.[28] In effect, they accepted the gaps as strategic policy but not as inviolable critical natural capital. Whilst the panel also accepted the case for restricting housing growth, the decision was challenged by central government which directed the county council to increase its housing numbers, something that it was reluctantly forced to do.

Whilst differentiating between critical and constant categories of capital is no longer a feature of planning policy, natural capital itself has seen a resurgence of interest following the UN Millennium Ecosystem Assessment (2005)[29] and the UK National Ecosystem Assessment (2011).[30] Since 2012, the UK Government has been advised by the Natural Capital Committee, chaired by Oxford University economist Dieter Helm. The concept has increasingly appeared in public policy documents since the establishment of this committee, for example, it is a core theme of the UK Government's 25 Year Environment Plan published in January 2018 (see Chapter 7).

Natural capital accounting, attempting to assess the value and costs associated with maintaining capital stocks, has also been promoted by governments and business corporations worldwide to complement financial accounting. The Department for Environment, Food and Rural Affairs (DEFRA) in England, for example, has initiated pilots looking at natural capital accounting in different contexts: urban conurbations (Greater Manchester – see Case Study 8); water catchments (Cumbria and Lancashire); landscapes (Devon); and the marine environment (east and west coast locations). There have also been pilots in corporate natural capital accounting. Tarmac, for example, is accounting for the value and benefits of natural capital at its Mancetter quarry in Warwickshire with the objective of making a 'net positive' contribution to biodiversity.

Case Study 8   **Natural capital accounting objectives for Greater Manchester** [31]

- Develop and test a communications and engagement model that brings together sectors, organisations and the public to deliver more for the environment.
- Develop a demonstrator project that shows the benefit of a natural capital approach on project funding.
- Create a Natural Capital Investment Plan for Greater Manchester.
- Demonstrate a 'place based' approach to delivery that improves policy and decision making.
- Cross cutting supporting action.

Ecosystem services

The principal focus of natural capital accounting is on the value of services that the natural environment provides for society. These are often called ecosystem services – services that are recognised to have economic value, but their value is often underestimated or even overlooked. *The UK National Ecosystem Assessment* noted that 'the benefits that we derive from the natural world and its constituent ecosystems are critically important to human well-being and economic prosperity but are consistently undervalued in economic analysis and decision making'.[32]

Ecosystem services can be described in simple terms as providing:

- Natural resources for basic survival such as clean air and water;
- Contribution to good physical and mental health, for example through access to green space, both urban and rural, and genetic resources for medicines;
- Natural processes such as climate regulation, flood and drought relief, and crop pollination;

- Support for a strong, healthy economy through industry and agriculture, or through tourism and recreation; and
- Social, cultural and educational benefits, well-being and inspiration from interaction with nature.

The UN Millennium Ecosystem Assessment set out a typology of ecosystem services under four headings which is also used in the UK assessment: provisioning services such as food and water; regulating services such as flood prevention, water quality and carbon sequestration; supporting services such as crop pollination; and cultural services such as recreation, health and well-being. National planning policy guidance in England indicates that the planning system should recognise the wider benefits of ecosystem services but does not specify how this might be achieved. DEFRA (2007)[33] suggests that ecosystem services could perhaps be addressed through policy appraisal systems such as Strategic Environmental Assessment (SEA) of plans and strategies and Environmental Impact Assessment (EIA) of development projects and proposals (see Chapter 6).

The economic value of ecosystem services is illustrated by Tony Juniper in his books: *What Has Nature Ever Done for Us?* (2012)[34] and *What Nature Does for Britain* (2015).[35] He estimates the annual value of Britain's ecosystem services amounts to £1.5 trillion. Putting an economic value on the natural environment is not without its critics; the very idea of putting a monetary value on beautiful landscapes and unique habitats is alien to many people. Juniper responds to that argument saying 'while it is quite right that not everything can be valued in purely financial terms (the beauty of a rare butterfly, for example), some elements of the natural world increasingly can be. It is crucial to make the point that nature has a real worth in economic terms.'[36] These concepts are beginning to be adopted to inform policy (see Case Study 9).

Noordwaard polder restoration[37]

Noordwaard is an area of 4,450ha bordering the Biesbosch national park in the Netherlands where the polder has been re-profiled and dykes breached to restore the floodplain as part of the Government's Space for Rivers Programme. The intention is to provide flood storage for the River Rhine and thus mitigate potential flooding downstream, in Rotterdam for example. Whilst it also includes extensive engineering works and some relocation of farms and homes, the project adopts a back-to-nature approach, creating a new landscape with space set aside for nature along the banks of restored streams and the flood channel. The polder used to be protected from flooding by a 23km-long levee. This was removed on the south side of the polder and, during high tides, water freely flows into creeks in the low-lying nature area. The nature area covers half of the polder and can be underwater for up to one hundred days per year, creating new wetland habitats which are valuable for overwintering and migratory wildfowl. Restoration of the floodplain provides climate change-related flood protection, improves environmental quality for people and nature, increases recreational facilities and boosts the economy.

Recognising the multiple benefits provided by ecosystem services, public policy decision makers increasingly search for multifunctional solutions, which address as many ecosystem services as possible at the same time. Examples include natural

←
Aerial view of Bowesfield, Teesside. These wetlands were created alongside commercial and housing developments.

flood management projects developed primarily for flood prevention that also create wildlife habitats, recreational opportunities and water purification (see Case Study 9 above). These are sometimes described as win-win-win solutions which maximise benefits arising from the development for the environment, society and the economy. Another excellent example of a win-win-win project can be found on the bank of the River Tees at Bowesfield in Stockton-on-Tees, where agreements between a developer, government agency, local planning authority and the local wildlife trust (Tees Valley Wildlife Trust) has enabled a development that provides employment, housing, gains for biodiversity, recreational opportunities and flood water management (see Case Study 43 in Chapter 6). A different, but equally beneficial, example of the multifunctional use of land can be found at Woodberry Wetlands (see Case Study 10) where an existing reservoir has been opened to the public as part of an urban regeneration project.

Case Study 10   **Woodberry Wetlands**

Woodberry Wetlands were created on a water supply reservoir constructed in 1833 and previously closed to the public. An agreement between Thames Water and London Wildlife Trust (LWT) in Hackney, London, allowed the Wildlife Trust to engage the local community in nearby Woodberry Down, an area undergoing redevelopment, in environmental enhancement works around the reservoir. These improvements included habitat creation (reedbeds and wildlife-rich grassland) and recreational access for the community (boardwalk and an access bridge). An at-risk listed building was also restored and

→
Woodberry Wetlands, London. The wetlands were developed as environmental enhancements with multiple benefits for the local community.

converted into a cafe as part of the scheme. Many local volunteers assisted in the works and continue to be engaged in the management of the wetlands. Contact with Berkley Homes, the developer engaged in the regeneration work and construction of additional houses, has enabled the Wildlife Trust to influence the landscaping of the Woodberry Down Estate, creating sustainable drainage swales and other features of ecological value.

—

Biodiversity offsetting

Linked to debates about natural capital are those associated with the concept of biodiversity offsetting. This is touted as a means of compensating for potential losses as a result of development. Whilst planners have had access to negotiating tools to secure developer contributions to offset biodiversity losses for many years (section 106 of the 1990 Town and Country Planning Act in England, for example), the technique of biodiversity offsetting appears to offer a more structured and transparent approach with a (arguably limited) track record of success in many countries throughout the world – in Australia, India, the United States and Germany for instance. Offsets are described by the Government in England as 'conservation activities designed to compensate for residual losses. They are different from other kinds of ecological compensation as they need to show measurable outcomes that are sustained over time.'[38] In other countries, markets have been established in biodiversity offsets which are banked and can be used to support habitat creation and enhancement elsewhere.

Crucial to offsetting schemes is the internationally accepted mitigation hierarchy:

- In the first instance harm should be avoided, for example by locating development at a different site;
- Where this is not possible the impacts should be minimised, for instance in the detailed design of the development;
- Lastly, any residual impacts should be compensated for, by restoring or recreating habitat elsewhere.

The hierarchy is important as it makes clear that offsetting is not a means of enabling development regardless of its environmental impact. Moreover, it emphasises that compensation should be a last resort, not a negotiating ploy to secure planning permission which might damage an important habitat. International Union for the Conservation of Nature (IUCN) policy on biodiversity offsets reinforces the importance of rigorously applying the mitigation hierarchy.

> Biodiversity offsets are intended to be carried out as the final step of the mitigation hierarchy – avoid, minimise, restore and offset – to help meet a scheme's environmental objectives. This implies they should only be applied to the residual project-specific impacts on biodiversity after appropriate efforts have been made first to avoid adverse impacts to biodiversity, then to minimise the unavoidable impacts, and finally to restore biodiversity on-site at the conclusion of a project.[39]

The process of biodiversity offsetting uses a metric to decide how much offsetting is required – in England a metric was devised for six pilot schemes which were begun in 2012 (see Case Study 11).

Case Study 11   **Biodiversity metric for England pilots**

The England pilots used a metric which quantifies the value of habitats based on three criteria:

- The **distinctiveness** of the habitat is assessed as low, medium or high. Distinctiveness reflects, amongst other factors, the rarity of the habitat concerned (at local, regional, national and international scales) and the degree to which it supports species rarely found in other habitats. Guidance has been provided alongside the pilot, setting out the distinctiveness rating for different habitat types.

- The **quality** of the habitat is assessed as poor, moderate or good. This assessment is based on a standard framework. In the pilots this has been Natural England's 'Higher-Level Stewardship: Farm Environment Plan (FEP) Manual'.

- The **area** of the habitat in hectares.

Having assessed the habitat against these factors, its value in 'biodiversity units' can be calculated using the following table: Offset providers use the same system to calculate the number of 'biodiversity units' they should provide, taking account of three additional factors:

Value of 1ha in 'biodiversity units'		Habitat distinctiveness		
		Low (2)	Medium (4)	High (6)
Habitat quality	Good (3)	6	12	18
	Moderate (2)	4	8	12
	Poor (1)	2	4	6

- The **risk** associated with habitat restoration or recreation, as not all activities will achieve the desired outcome. An offset provider may need to restore or recreate a larger area to have confidence that the required number of 'biodiversity units' will be created. For the offset pilots, restoration and recreation activities have been classified in four bands from low to very high difficulty. For low difficulty sites, no increase in area is required. For very high difficulty restoration or recreation activity, ten times as much area will need to be improved to generate the same number of 'biodiversity units'.

- The **time** it will take to restore or recreate the habitat. In this period society will experience a net loss of biodiversity, so the system can require the offset provider to do more to compensate for this temporary loss. In the pilots this is handled by applying a 3.5% discount rate as set out in HM Treasury's Green Book.

- The **location** of the offset. In the pilots local authorities have set out strategies on where to locate offsets to create maximum environmental gain. Larger offsets need to be provided if they are outside the area identified for offset provision.[40]

There has been considerable debate about whether the aim of biodiversity offsetting should be 'no net loss', i.e. that existing (and historically much depleted) levels of biodiversity should be maintained, or 'net gain', representing enhancement of biological capital. In both cases there are issues of what baseline net gain and no net loss should be measured against, and also at what time in the future would be appropriate to decide whether it has been achieved or not. Even so, there is little consensus amongst existing offsetting schemes about which of these objectives should be pursued and some have changed from one to the other. The African Development Bank, for example, has an objective that its support 'should deliver a net benefit or no net loss for residual biodiversity impacts on natural habitats'.[41] In Victoria, Australia, the objective of offsetting shifted from achieving net gains for native vegetation to no net loss because, amongst other things, of difficulties arising in trying to achieve and justify gains (see Case Study 12).

The English Government's NPPF opts for securing net gains for biodiversity 'minimising impacts on biodiversity and providing net gains wherever possible, contributing to the Government's commitment to halt the overall decline in biodiversity'.[42] However, whilst the aim might be net gain, the phrase 'wherever possible' introduces a significant loophole for developers. Developing a high-speed railway between London and the Midlands and North has proved to be extremely controversial not least because HS2 Ltd have opted for a policy of no net loss in calculating mitigation and compensation for its considerable impacts on biodiversity. Even so, it has conceded that there will in fact be a deficit in biodiversity units associated with the development. Environmental organisations also criticise the lack of attention being paid to connectivity between habitats that will be fragmented by the railway. In early 2018, discussions were being held about creating a green corridor to help reduce the impact on the environment, support wildlife and integrate the railway into the environment. This approach, though an improvement on previous strategy, takes little account of connections outside the rail corridor. Lack of consideration of habitat connectivity and impact on ecosystem services are issues that arise in many biodiversity offsetting schemes. In contrast, a biodiversity offsetting scheme associated with renewable energy developments in the Scottish Borders appears to be having positive outcomes (see Case Study 13).[43]

Biodiversity offsetting, Victoria, Australia[44]

In Australia, the state of Victoria has had legislation in place to control clearance of native vegetation since 1989. In 2002, it issued detailed guidance on how to achieve this, including mitigation and compensation through biodiversity offsets with an overall aim to achieve net gains for biodiversity. Like many similar schemes, it identified a common unit of measurement – habitat hectares – as the basis for offsetting, which was calculated by taking into account the area of habitat that would be lost, its quality and context (scarcity, links with wider ecosystems and its importance for wildlife).

After ten years of offsetting, Victoria decided to modify its approach by issuing new guidelines and shifting the aim of the scheme from net gain for biodiversity to no net loss, which would appear to indicate a lowering of aspirations for the conservation of native vegetation. There were many problems with the original scheme including that the objectives were not clearly understood, it was expensive to operate, it lacked transparency, there was poor compliance and poor enforcement processes, and a lack of strategic planning. But there were also issues common to many other offsetting schemes:

- Applicants for permission believed that ecological constraints could always be overcome by offsetting and as a result compensation became the default position rather than a last resort;

- In many cases, the offsets also failed to provide the expected biodiversity gains, often being scattered and at some distance from the development site, losing connectivity with similar sites and ecological networks; and

- Monitoring the offset sites proved difficult and expensive resulting in objectives being missed.

Scottish Borders biodiversity offsetting scheme

Biodiversity offsetting in the Scottish Borders arose as a response to the significant number of renewable energy developments taking place. Of particular concern were wind farms in the uplands, which were impacting on sensitive habitats such as blanket bog and upland heath which can support populations of black grouse, a protected species. The Scottish Borders local development plan requires wind farm developers to demonstrate that they have considered options for minimising impacts. The aim is to mitigate impacts

↑
Black grouse.

on site but if this is not possible it allows offsets to be positioned in proximity to the development.

The first offset was developed in 2006 and related to a wind farm development and its impact on black grouse. Since then, further schemes have been delivered through several different programmes. As a result, biodiversity offsetting is now an integral part of the planning process and embedded in planning policy and development plans. Developers are required to deliver compensatory habitat as well as direct mitigation measures. In seeking biodiversity benefits at a landscape scale, wider benefits accrue, including those for ecosystem services – flood protection, water quality, carbon storage and recreation. Habitat targets have been exceeded whilst offsets have supported two black grouse projects which between them have put more than 30,000ha of black grouse habitat under positive management for grouse.

Professional bodies representing ecologists and environmental managers (CIRIA, CIEEM and IEMA) have cooperated in identifying principles which should be addressed in offsetting:[45]

- Apply the mitigation hierarchy;
- Avoid losing biodiversity that cannot be compensated for elsewhere;
- Be inclusive and equitable – achieve net gain in partnership with stakeholders where possible;
- Address risks – mitigate difficulty, uncertainty and other risks;
- Make a measurable net gain contribution;
- Achieve the best outcome for biodiversity;
- Be additional – achieve outcomes that exceed obligations;
- Create a net gain legacy;
- Optimise sustainability;
- Be transparent.

Additionally, Town and Country Planning Association and The Wildlife Trusts recommend that offset gains should be planned as part of ecological networks, as isolated sites are unlikely to provide long-term net gains. They should also aim to provide equivalent or improved ecosystem services.[46] Detailed international guidance on biodiversity has been issued by IUCN,[47] which also calls for the application of the precautionary principle at all stages in the process.

Conclusions

Whilst approaches to environmental sustainability have evolved over the last twenty years, this chapter illustrates how many of the issues debated in the past remain the same issues facing planners today. In particular, planners still wrestle with issues including:

- How to mitigate damaging development and compensate for environmental losses?
- How to assess the capacity of locations to accommodate further development?
- How to identify thresholds beyond which environmental limits will be breached?
- What aspects of the environment, if any, should be given absolute protection from development?

- What value should be attached to different environmental assets?
- How to plan natural green space which satisfies multiple objectives?

Nevertheless, as illustrated in the case studies, advances have been made in tackling some of these issues. Moreover, the issues are now much more widely recognised and incorporated into national planning policy and practice guidance.

Introduction

In Chapter 1, the five main drivers of wildlife decline in Britain
were set out, namely unsustainable development that destroys
habitat, agricultural intensification, resource depletion (especially
industrial fishing), atmospheric nitrogen pollution and human-
induced climate change. As a result of better development
control, in turn resulting from stronger nature conservation
legislation and more effective planning guidance, the destruction
of SSSIs has almost ceased. River pollution has fallen
considerably as sewage works have become more efficient
and the Environment Agency has regulated against the worst
point source polluters. On farmed land, whilst agricultural
intensification continues apace, at least existing high-quality
habitat is often positively managed for its wildlife and
environmental value through the rural development policies of
CAP. And yet, wildlife continues to decline, especially those
species that depend on particular habitats (rather than
generalists whose numbers are increasing in some cases).
The reason for this decline can be explained by the theory of
island biogeography.

Island biogeography

The science of island biogeography has a long pedigree. Darwin
famously formulated the origin of species through the study of
finches on the Galapagos Islands; Wallace paralleled thinking on
evolution by studying islands in what is now Indonesia, famously
describing the 'Wallace line' between Bali and Sulawesi that

separates two distinct sets of fauna. However, the landmark paper was initially published in 1963 by MacArthur and Wilson[48] and the theory was further extended in a book of 1967.[49] Here, the authors showed why larger and less isolated islands have greater diversity than smaller, more isolated islands. In essence, less isolated (closer to the mainland) islands are colonised by more species, while smaller islands suffer from local extinctions because the habitat 'patches' that support those species are smaller and the species populations themselves are smaller, making them more vulnerable to ecosystem change, such as disease, natural and human-caused disaster (flood, drought, disturbance, extreme temperatures and climate change generally).

A famous example illustrates the theory. Before 1598, there were no humans living on the island of Mauritius in the Indian Ocean. Dutch sailors who settled on the island after 1598 described a large flightless pigeon-like bird that was unafraid of humans, very easy to hunt and made for good eating. By 1662, all the dodos had been killed on Mauritius and, given it was an island endemic (only found on Mauritius), the bird became extinct. Other island-living flightless birds have not (yet) become extinct. For example, in New Zealand the five species of kiwi, though threatened, remain in existence because there were far more of them originally (New Zealand is far larger than Mauritius) and some of the habitat they thrive in remains.

So far, so obvious, but the profound implications of this theory on species extinctions was not fully examined until 1985, by Wilcox and Murphy.[50] They showed that fragmentation of habitat (the creation of 'islands' of habitat) drives species extinction because it reduces the 'patch' area of suitable habitat. Fragmentation increasingly isolates species, thus reducing the possibility of recolonisation should a particular species go locally extinct in that particular patch of habitat. Additionally, fragmentation creates more 'edge' habitat that is suboptimal for a species that thrives in a particular habitat. Many nature reserves have in effect become 'islands' in a 'sea' of intensively farmed countryside and urban development. As such they suffer from the same threats as offshore islands. Fragmentation drives species extinction locally (see Case Study 14), which eventually adds up to global extinction, especially when the patches of remaining habitat are small.

Species are becoming extinct today at the fastest rate ever known in the history of life on Earth, leading some to name the current period the Sixth Great Age of Extinction[51] or the Anthropocene.[52]

———

Case Study 14

The local extinction of small blue butterfly at Old Burghclere lime quarry

To illustrate the implications of island biogeography, we could examine the fate of the small blue butterfly at Old Burghclere lime quarry in Hampshire. This Hampshire and Isle of Wight Wildlife Reserve is an old quarry famed for its rich flora and its butterflies, including the now rather rare small blue butterfly. Despite good management of the reserve by the Wildlife Trust, small blue became extinct at the site in 2003. This was because the neighbouring farmer had complained about rabbits from the reserve eating his crops, forcing the Wildlife Trust to fence in the rabbits which in turn led to severe overgrazing by rabbits. Over time, this would not really matter as rabbit populations go up and down, especially when myxomatosis gets hold. Unfortunately, in this case, the rabbits grazed out the food plant of the small blue butterfly, the kidney vetch. Again, taking a

↓
Small blue on
kidney vetch.

longer-term view, this should not really matter, as once the rabbit numbers declined, the kidney vetch would bloom again and allow small blue to recolonise the site. At Old Burghclere, however, it is 9.5km to the nearest small blue population (at the rabbit-famed Watership Down) across an intensive arable landscape. For a small blue butterfly such a flight is impossible and thus they became locally extinct. For many species, the same process has led to complete British extinction. As agriculture intensifies and fragmentation increases, local species extinctions continue – both the numbers of individuals and species diversity continue an inexorable decline.

If habitat fragmentation drives local and ultimately species extinction, then reconnecting habitats should do the opposite and drive the restoration of species abundance and diversity, at least for those remaining species. Ergo, the creation of larger habitat patches (which increases the ratio of core to edge habitat) by connecting habitat patches together and creating new stepping-stone habitats, should enable species to be more resilient to ecosystem changes such as prolonged drought, cold, wet weather, fire and so on. If species numbers do fall, then connected habitats are more able to be recolonised, ensuring that local extinctions are temporary. Moreover, if ecosystem change is permanent (for example, climate change results in a permanently warmer climate), then species can, through step-wise colonisation, move in response to these changing environmental conditions. Already, mobile species such as birds and some insects are moving to suitable habitat as the warming trend of climate is locked in. Speckled Wood butterfly was once a southern England specialist but is now regularly seen as far north as Scotland. For less mobile species (for example, trees that can only 'move' through seedlings growing in more suitable locations), well connected habitat is essential given rapid climate change.

This lies at the heart of *Making Space for Nature*, a report submitted to Government in 2010. The 'bigger, better, more and connected' mantra from the Lawton committee is no soundbite, rather a considered response to the theory of island biogeography. Lawton et al. set out the approach:

Ecological networks have become widely recognised as an effective response to conserve wildlife in environments that have become fragmented by human activities. An ecological network comprises a suite of high quality sites which collectively contain the diversity and area of habitat that are needed to support species, and which have ecological connections between them that enable species, or at least their genes, to move.[53]

This is explained graphically in the figure below

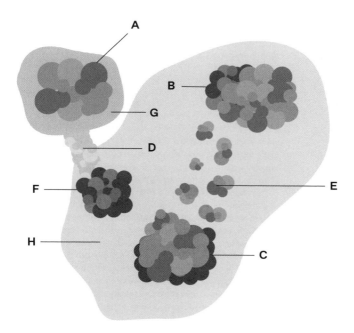

↑
Components of an ecological network. Redrawn after Lawton et al. *Making Space for Nature.*

Approaches include: improving the quality of habitat patches (a); by making existing habitat patches bigger (b), which can include creating ecotones – the transition between or blending of two different habitats (c); enhancing connectivity through a continuous corridor (d) or a stepping-stone (e); creating new sites (f); and reducing pressure on sites either by establishing buffer zones (g) or enhancing the wider environment (h).

Towards bigger habitat patches

Given this ecological theory, conservationists argue for and attempt to develop larger and more connected areas of land in which wildlife can thrive.

Island biogeographical theory shows that larger patches are more resilient to change. For example, in the Amazon rainforest, researchers measured the biodiversity of various sized patches of remaining habitat, demonstrating that larger patch sizes contained greater abundance and diversity of species.[54] Given this, there is a desire to create larger conservation areas. In Cambridgeshire, for example, a partnership of the local Wildlife Trust, the local authority and government agencies came together to link two of the few remaining fragments of fenland back together through an exceptionally ambitious large-scale project known as the Great Fen (see Case Study 15).

Case Study 15   **Great Fen project**

Fens once stretched for hundreds of miles across Eastern England, home to beavers, otters and many other types of animals and plants. When the land was drained with an elaborate system of ditches and river diversions in the seventeenth century, more than 99% of this wild habitat disappeared. The reclaimed land has been farmed since then, but the peat soils are fragile, and the land has been shrinking and the soils eroding.

Two remaining fragments of fen habitat can be found south of Peterborough in Cambridgeshire. Woodwalton Fen and Holme Fen are both managed as National Nature Reserves but are threatened because they are too small and isolated to maintain their biodiversity value which has been progressively declining. The Great Fen Partnership conceived a project to dramatically extend these habitats through an ambitious habitat creation programme that will eventually connect the two sites back together in a mosaic of wetland, grassland and wet woodland. This requires the creation of 3,750ha of restored fen landscape between Huntingdon and Peterborough. At the heart of this strategy is restoration of existing habitats and habitat creation. In so doing, the strategy will improve access and enjoyment, foster socio-economic development, especially through nature tourism, and contribute to climate change adaptation and mitigation.

The Great Fen Masterplan, published in 2010, sets out how the Great Fen project will recreate and restore ancient fenland

↑
Construction
of new wetlands
as part of the
Great Fen
project.

landscape over the coming years and decades and how it will
deliver a wide range of benefits for the surrounding area.
Included in the strategy are plans for:

- Mosaic of wildlife habitats to support a variety of fen species;

- Visitor facilities, including a cafe, trails, natural play areas
  and events;

- New footpaths, cycleways and bridleways linking to local
  communities;

- Areas to store floodwater during high rainfall, to help protect
  surrounding farmland and communities; and

- Zones to encourage access to some areas but protect the
  most sensitive areas from heavy disturbance.

Despite the project comprising a 50-year vision and starting
only in 2001, by 2017 more than half of the total area was being
managed for nature conservation; avocets and common crane
have already returned to the Great Fen after a 400-year
absence. In 2010, the project won the Royal Town Planning
Institute's prestigious Silver Cup.

Towards more connected habitats

A reconnection of habitats is becoming increasingly critical as climate change takes hold. At the end of the last Ice Age, temperate vegetation recolonised the former British tundra and ice fields from the refugia in southern Europe as the temperature rose. Colonising trees such as birch and willow were eventually replaced by pine and then by oak-ash-lime woodlands – a gradual northward colonisation taking place over many hundreds of years.[55] Mobile species, of course, moved much faster. Such a warming episode is once again in play, this time created by humans whose activities have elevated greenhouse gases, such as carbon dioxide, in the atmosphere. Species colonisation today though is much more difficult as much of the human-modified landscape is deeply hostile to many species of wildlife. A critical element of the Lawton et al. approach is to create corridors and stepping stones, which they note as

> spaces that improve the functional connectivity between core areas, enabling species to move between them to feed, disperse, migrate or reproduce. Connectivity need not come from linear, continuous habitats; a number of small sites may act as 'stepping stones' across which certain species can move between core areas. Equally, a land mosaic between sites that allows species to move is effectively an ecological corridor.[56]

Linear infrastructure causes particular barriers to ecological connectivity. One way to mitigate the impact of these barriers is to build green bridges (see Case Study 16).

Case Study 16 **Scotney Castle green bridge**

In Kent, a proposed new dual carriageway to bypass Lamberhurst village near Tunbridge Wells risked fragmenting the High Weald Area of Natural Beauty. The scheme threatened to sever the historic West Drive dating from 1842 that is used as the main entrance to the National Trust-owned Scotney Castle. National Trust worked with the Highways Agency to develop a 'Landbridge' that enabled the West Drive to be reinstated on its original line and provided landscape and habitat

→
Dormouse.

connectivity. A particular concern was the disconnection of
dormouse communities, so habitats on the bridge were
designed to encourage dormice and nesting boxes were
installed. Surveys have shown that dormice do indeed use
the bridge, with breeding dormice recorded living on the
bridge itself.

—

Towards landscape-scale nature conservation
Developing conservation priorities based on an ecological
network, along the lines proposed by Lawton et al., can be
approached through the development of ecological opportunity
maps. One approach is to use modelling techniques to analyse
a 'least-cost' development of an ecological network.[57] This
confers a degree of objectivity to the development of a proposed
ecological network. Another approach is to use 'by-eye'
interpretation and best judgement to consider where ecological
networks are practically most possible to achieve. For example,
Yorkshire Wildlife Trust produced its proposed ecological network
Living Landscapes map by mapping all semi-natural habitat,
printing it out on large-scale maps and then inviting experts to
set out where it would be most likely to create wildlife-rich,
ecologically well-connected landscapes within a 50-year
timeframe (assuming a favourable political environment for
nature conservation).[58] The two approaches give surprisingly

similar results whilst the latter has the benefit of adding in the extra potential of habitat creation relating to an area's peculiar circumstances (for example, the likelihood of managed realignment of a coastline at a particular location). In Holland, the Government produced the Dutch Nature Policy Plan following a similar approach (see Case Study 17).

Case Study 17   **The Dutch Nature Policy Plan**

In 1990, the Dutch Government adopted the Dutch Nature Policy Plan. At the heart of this programme was the development of the Dutch Ecological Network[59] – with an aim to have 728,500ha of nature reserve, designated sites and nature corridors in place by 2025 that together would create an ecological network that addresses the issue of habitat fragmentation, especially in the light of climate change. High land prices, reduced commitment to the plan by the national Government and a weakening of the institutions responsible for this plan, especially the closure of the Rural Land Exchange, has meant that the network is unlikely to be achieved by the target date. Nevertheless, the initiative has led to some remarkable interventions, such as the development of Oostvaardersplassen (see Case Study 29 in Chapter 4).

←
Sustainable drainage installed in a school in South Yorkshire.

A different take on landscape-scale conservation action is seen in England's approach to meeting the terms of the European Water Framework Directive. The Directive requires member states to ensure that all water bodies achieve 'good ecological and chemical status',[60] and the actions required to achieve such status must be set out within River Basin Management Plans, first published in the UK in 2009. The River Basin Plans generally cover Britain's bigger catchments or a group of catchments – the Severn, the Thames, the Humber, the Dee, Northumbria, South West England, etc.

Resolving some of the issues set out within these Plans requires more local coordination of action. To facilitate this, the Environment Agency developed catchment partnerships, hosted by external partners such as Rivers Trusts and Wildlife Trusts and covering particular river catchments. England now has over one hundred catchment partnerships in operation, which take what they describe as 'a community-led approach that engages people and groups from across society to help improve our precious water environments'.[61]

For example, the Torne River Catchment Partnership has developed its vision and strategy for bringing the river into 'good ecological and chemical status' working directly with

→
Construction of dams to slow in-channel flow, contributing to a reduction in downstream flooding and improving river water quality.

13 different partners including the Environment Agency, NGOs, local authorities and internal drainage boards. The strategy for 'our hardworking river' sets out the challenge of its poor water quality and then describes how the partnership will attempt to address these issues and what mechanisms it might use to help.[62] These range from talking to individual farmers to reduce soil erosion into the stream into to working with local schools to install small-scale sustainable drainage schemes – as much to engage children in the catchment approach as to reduce diffuse pollution into the Torne.

Likewise, in the Aire Catchment under the auspices of the Aire and Calder Partnership, work is under way to improve water quality in the upper catchment by reducing siltation into upper tributaries. The methods used (see Case Study 18) also reduce water flow to and within the stream and can reduce storm flood peaks. This work is being expanded to help reduce flooding in urban areas following smaller-scale pilots (see Case Study 19).

Case Study 18   **Improving water quality in the River Aire**

Industrialisation of the River Aire valley in West Yorkshire from the seventeenth century dramatically affected the river. Weirs, used for water power, stopped fish migration whilst pollution from the mills that lined the river eventually led to most of the river being functionally dead. From the 1970s, efforts to stop point source pollution of the river allied to deindustrialisation and efforts to build fish passages to bypass weirs have dramatically improved the ecology of the river. From a dead river in the 1970s, otters are now occasionally seen in the middle of Leeds. However, water quality still does not meet the stricter requirements of the Water Framework Directive, often due to diffuse pollution from agriculture.

To resolve these issues, land advisors are working with farmers to introduce simple measures to reduce silt getting into the river system. Fencing off bank-sides from cattle to reduce poaching, building in-channel woody debris dams to trap silt in the river and slow the flow, and building in-field leaky dams to slow the flow from hillsides to the stream and thus reduce erosion are all deployed.

Slowing the flow in Pickering Beck

Following a series of floods in Pickering, a small town in North Yorkshire, various investigations were undertaken to understand the cost–benefit ratio of installing new flood defences. Traditional hard flood defences had a low cost–benefit ratio, so a completely different approach to flood management was trialled in which the hydrology of the whole catchment was modelled to see if floodwaters could be stored above the town to resolve flooding – natural flood management. Various approaches were taken: the installation of large woody debris dams, the construction of leaky timber bunds across the floodplain, blocking moorland grips, establishing no-burn moorland buffer strips to increase surface roughness, planting farm, riparian and floodplain woodland, and farm-scale measures such as installing sediment ponds, swales and check dams, cross drains on tracks and small-scale storage.

The catchments of the two main tributaries of Pickering Beck received different treatments. In one, rather cheap leaky dams, woody debris dams and woodland planting was undertaken. In the other, a much larger and far more expensive flood storage scheme was developed by building an earthen bank. The system was fully tested during Storm Eva on Boxing Day in 2015 where Pickering did not flood.[63] Notably, the cheaper treatment, using natural flood management solutions, worked just as well as the more expensive engineered scheme.

Part of the work of the Pickering flood defence project (see Case Study 19) was to block moorland 'grips' (drains) that were mostly dug into upland blanket bogs in an attempt to improve grazing and funded through agricultural subsidy systems. Gripping of upland blanket bog is remarkably extensive across the UK. In Yorkshire alone, the Yorkshire Peat Partnership has mapped over 5,800km of drainage ditches. Where the drainage system directs water into particular grips erosion is rapid, and grips erode into substantial gullies. By blocking these systems, the flow of water from upland moor to the streams is slowed thereby reducing flood peaks.[64]

Restoration of peatlands, through ditch blocking, re-vegetation with more characteristic species, gully re-profiling and blocking, returns peatlands from a source to a sink of atmospheric carbon.[65] Given that peatlands contain twice as much carbon as woodlands on just 3% of the world's land-surface, they represent Earth's most important store of carbon. Damage to peatlands, especially in North America, Europe and South East Asia, means that peatlands contribute 5 to 8% of all human-caused emission of carbon to the atmosphere. Restoring peatlands is considered by many to be one of the most cost-effective ways of reducing carbon emissions to the atmosphere.

—

Planning as a tool to create ecological networks

Using better land management to resolve issues such as water quality, flooding and climate change links to the concept of ecosystem services outlined in more detail in Chapter 2. Likewise, that chapter notes that many of these services, though valuable to society, are not represented in the marketplace. A land manager of a peatland in the Pennines, for example, is not paid by anyone to sequester carbon from the atmosphere and as a result it does not figure in their business approach to land management. It is often the case that common public 'goods' (benefits) to society are difficult to value within the context of a free market. For example, whilst it may be 'free' to walk into an urban park, it is still valuable to those users. As a result, society protects those urban green spaces through regulation (in this case, the planning system) and pays for the cost of maintaining parks through local taxation.

Whilst the planning system is named 'Town and Country Planning', in practice its reach is significantly constrained outside the built environment. Indeed, some agricultural developments are exempt from development control planning through permitted development rights.

Rural land-use planning, therefore, is mainly controlled by other forms of regulation. For example, the protection of species and habitats is controlled by environmental law through the designation of SSSI, Special Protection Areas (SPAs) and Special Conservation Areas (see Chapter 1). Another example is nitrate vulnerable zones, where land managers are required to restrict nitrogen run-off from fertilisers or slurries. There are further controls to protect drinking water catchments. However, these

designations have a limited scope and are not designed to maintain or enhance the many different beneficial ecosystem services a landscape can provide. For example, blanket bog above Sheffield provides a recreational landscape for walkers and grouse shooters, a very significant store of carbon, a reservoir of unusual wildlife, a rough surface to slow the flow from hilltop rain to urban drain and is the source
of Sheffield's drinking water. Yet only the wildlife present in the landscape is recognised in any designation.

The Natural Capital Committee of the UK Government recognises this weakness, challenging the 2017 Conservative Government to act upon its commitment 'of being the first generation to leave the natural environment of England in a better state than that in which we found it'.[66] The Committee recommends that the Government puts the 25 Year Environment Plan[67] on a statutory footing. Likewise, environmental NGOs are calling for a new Environment Act[68] that requires Government to spatially map ecosystem services and require public policy to protect and, where possible, enhance those services. Under this proposal, the planning system would identify green and wild spaces and then design housing and development around them, along with ways to reconnect and recreate habitats where needed. A commitment to the creation of ecological networks would be a goal of all applicable public policy, including public investment, planning and advice.

The Natural Capital Committee notes that 'the impending exit of the UK from the EU provides an opportunity to undertake a more fundamental review of how government supports the protection and improvement of the natural environment'.[69] This is picked up by the 25 Year Environment Plan in which there is a clear commitment to ensure that public policy 'will move to a system of paying farmers public money for public goods . . . (with the) . . . the principal public good . . . (as) . . . environmental enhancement'.[70] The plan also sets out a commitment to 'embed an "environmental net gain" principle for development, including housing and infrastructure' (see Chapter 7).[71]

If these commitments are fed through into revised public policy, then the implications could be profound. A reversal of agricultural policy to ensure that fiscal intervention is used to secure public benefits such as the development of an ecological network to reverse fragmentation and a reformation of the planning system to ensure a net environmental gain whenever development is proposed offers the tantalising possibility that England could finally stop and reverse the decline of wildlife. In so doing, England would begin to enhance all those ecosystem services underpinned by its wildlife and natural environment – soil health, flood management, climate change mitigation, easy to treat raw water for drinking and, above all, wildlife-rich urban and rural green space for active play and recreation. The Natural Capital Committee call these ambitious, long-term outcomes from natural capital 'The Prize'. A prize indeed.

Chapter 4

Rebuilding Biodiversity

Introduction

In the last chapter, the prize of creating a wildlife-rich ecological network was set out. Some of that network is, of course, already in place. Across the UK, there is a network of wildlife-rich sites. Some of these are protected via designation (see Chapter 1), some protected through the planning system as Local Wildlife Sites and much not protected at all. In some parts of the country, especially in the arable lowlands, this network is highly fragmented and patchy. In others, semi-natural habitat (no habitat in the UK is truly natural) patches are far larger and better connected, especially in the uplands, on the coast and along some rivers. As the Lawton Review[72] makes clear, nowhere in England is the network adequate to stop species decline.

As a result, Lawton et al. recommend that policy and fiscal intervention is focused on creating an ecological network that can cope with the onslaught of climate change. There are three broad components to this approach: the management of existing habitat to maintain its quality; habitat restoration to improve its quality; and habitat creation to both expand and connect the network. A fourth component could be added – *rewilding*: allowing natural processes the room to create the network for us.

Habitat maintenance

Britain is a cultural landscape, by which we mean the landscape is a product of its natural *and* cultural history. The high moorlands of the Pennines are considered by many to be a beautiful natural scene but there is little natural about that scene. Pollen evidence shows that much of the British uplands was once covered in broad-leafed woodland,[73] though the form and openness of that woodland is open to conjecture.[74] Deforestation during the Neolithic and particularly the Bronze Age allied to climatic deterioration at the end of the Bronze Age led to soil degradation to form podzol soils and blanket peats, with domestic sheep and cattle grazing maintaining the open landscape so characteristic of the British uplands.

Likewise, most characteristic British habitats are cultural, the product of past management regimes. Meadows are sustained by cutting in the early summer, to provide hay for overwintering domestic animals, and after-cutting grazing during the late summer and autumn. Flower-rich woodlands are the product of coppicing (regular cutting back of recent growth to ground level) and pollarding (cropping of timber 2–3m off the ground), which have been deployed in our woodlands for thousands of years. Upland heaths are a product of burning and grazing and so on. Hoskins, in his seminal book the *Making of the English Landscape*,[75] combined the disciplines of ecology, history and geography to show how the countryside has developed over the last few thousand years. He sets out the markers within a landscape of that history – the pattern of fields, woods and settlements, for example. Likewise, Rackham[76] showed that many British woodlands have been in a similar form for hundreds of years, used for timber, coppice products and, in the industrial heartlands, for the charcoal that fuelled the early Industrial

←
Coppice
woodland
flowers at
Hetchell Wood,
Yorkshire.

Revolution. Most British hedgerows are not the last remnants of the 'wildwood', rather they were deliberately planted to enclose the open fields of the medieval period and through land enclosures under Acts of Parliament in the eighteenth and nineteenth centuries. In places, a ridge and furrow pattern can still be seen within these enclosed fields – the history of human-modified landscape change is all around us.

As such, many of our most characteristic wildlife species are the product of this cultural landscape. Dartford warblers thrive on lowland heaths with gorse – habitat created by Neolithic and Bronze Age farmers and sustained by thousands of years of grazing. Geese flock to the UK in winter to feast on natural estuarine vegetation and cultural planted grass in farmers' fields. The summer haze of meadow flowers is utterly dependent on continued cutting and grazing – traditional management stretching back over the millennia. The open landscape of the iconic white cliffs of Dover is an agricultural landscape, rather than a natural landscape. Not too surprisingly, nature conservation organisations often default to traditional agricultural techniques to manage such characteristic wildlife (see Case Study 20).

———

Case Study 20   **Wheldrake Ings**

Ings is a Viking word for wet meadows. These were highly beneficial in pre-industrial farming economies as wet meadows provided livestock with an 'early bite', allowing farmers to get their livestock to market ahead of others at much higher prices. Wetter meadows are warmed in early spring by high water levels flowing across the land, allowing grasses to come out of winter dormancy quicker than on neighbouring higher ground. One such site is Wheldrake Ings – a Yorkshire Wildlife Trust reserve a few kilometres south of York. Here, the land has been managed in a similar way for at least a thousand years. In winter, a swollen River Derwent spills across the floodplain to deposit a layer of fine nutrient-rich silt, with the waters attracting many thousands of wetland birds. As the waters drain away, the meadows grow quickly providing a rich crop of hay and after-cutting grazing to sustain domestic livestock. These lowland floodplain meadows would once have been extremely common in English river valleys but have now been largely drained for arable agriculture or converted to 'improved' (i.e. fertilised) rye-grass silage and pasture. Today, Wheldrake Ings forms one of the largest extents of floodplain meadow in the UK. Management is focused on maintaining the traditional agricultural system to conserve this habitat despite the fact that the market-based economic rationale has now largely ceased.

→
Lowland
floodplain
meadows at
Wheldrake Ings.

Habitat restoration

Since the Second World War, fertilisers and pesticides have allowed farmers to substantially increase productivity. For example, the Department for Environment, Food and Rural Affairs shows that British wheat yields averaged about 2.5 tonnes per hectare up to the Second World War. From then, they steadily rose, averaging about 8 tonnes per hectare today.[77] Industrial farming methods that increased yields, alongside tax-payer income support to farmers, have encouraged farmers to bring more land into arable production. Pastoral land has also been intensified. Hay meadows have largely been replaced by fertilised monocultures of fast growing rye-grass used for silage. On some of the most marginal soils agriculture has been replaced by state-sponsored forestry, either directly through the Forestry Commission or through various types of woodland grant scheme. And everywhere land drainage has been encouraged by state support, either through grants or through collective and state-sponsored action for flood defence or through Internal Drainage Boards.

As a result, much habitat has either been destroyed or substantially modified. Where habitat is modified, restoration may be possible. Examples include the restoration of drained peatlands (Case Study 21), forestry over felled ancient woodland (Case Study 22) and the restoration of rivers (Case Study 23).

Case Study 21   **Restoration of peatlands**

Globally blanket bog is globally a rare habitat relying on unusual climatic conditions where summer and winter temperatures are cool and vary little and there are over 150 rain-days per year.[78] Yorkshire is blessed with such a cool and wet climate and has about 70,200ha of blanket bog containing 38 million tonnes of carbon in the peat soils. However, most of this bog is damaged through drainage, atmospheric pollution and burning such that Yorkshire's peatlands, in common with peatlands across the UK, are now a source rather than a sink for atmospheric carbon. The Yorkshire Peat Partnership has used aerial photography to map this damage on blanket bog in the Pennines north of the River Calder and on the North York Moors. This reveals around 5,800km of drainage ditches (grips). Some of these ditches have eroded into substantial gullies and the bogs are now scarred with 1,800km of gully whilst fires have in places completely removed vegetation to leave 340ha of bare peat – this is a highly damaged ecosystem.

The Partnership of moorland owners and managers, state agencies and NGOs are working together to restore blanket

→
Helicopter dropping heather and sphagnum brash over damaged blanket bog in the Yorkshire Dales.

bog. Whilst discussion is ongoing on the role of burning for restoration management, there is a clear consensus to restore hydrology and vegetation through ditch blocking, gully re-profiling and establishing new vegetation.

From 2009 to March 2017, the Partnership secured and invested £15.1 million to restore blanket bog, surveying 38,000ha, undertaking restoration works on 27,000ha and in so doing blocking 1,850km of grips and 180km of gullies deploying about 130,000 dams. Sediment traps (using timber, heather bales and stone) have been installed in over 100km of gullies alongside re-profiling and re-vegetation of 1,680km of grips and 1,500km of gully-edges and hags.

Case Study 22   **Restoration of Milkwellburn Wood**

This woodland, managed as a Durham Wildlife Trust Nature Reserve since 2010, is typical of plantation over ancient woodland (PAWS) in that much of the woodland had previously been felled and planted with conifers. The remnants of ancient woodland are still found on the steeper slopes where the original woodland remains. Here, the ancient woodland is dominated by oak and ash with locally rare small-leaved lime and an understory of hazel, holly and honeysuckle. The ground flora includes plant species that are typical of ancient woodland such as greater woodrush, primrose, bluebell, dog's mercury, broad-leaved helleborine and many ferns such as hart's-tongue and lady fern.

Sensitive removal of conifers, using approaches such as continuous cover forestry, enables ancient woodland to re-establish, especially if, as at Milkwellburn Wood, some of the species associated with ancient woodlands can still be found. In this way they are able to recolonise the woodland restored through conifer removal.[79] Restoration of the woods is a long-term project spanning several decades, requiring the felling of non-native conifer species and replanting, or encouraging, natural regeneration of native species such as oak, ash and birch. This will create a more diverse woodland structure allowing light into the woodland floor, in turn promoting the growth of woodland wildflowers.

Case Study 23   **Restoration of the River Itchen, Winnall Moors**

Winnall Moors Nature Reserve is famed for both its ancient water meadows and its chalk river. Indeed, this was the site where dry-fly fishing was invented by G. Skues in the early twentieth century. Part of the site was bought by Hampshire and Isle of Wight Wildlife Trust who eventually took control of the carriers (channels) of the River Itchen where they crossed the reserve. This was not without controversy as the Trust ended the lease of a long-established fishing club on this part of the river. The Trust ended this lease because the river was, by then, being managed in a way that had degraded its special interest. Frequent dredging of weed, embankment of the riversides and removal of bankside vegetation had combined to create straight silted-up carriers that could only be fished through frequent stocking.

The Trust built a partnership with the local angling community to restore and manage the river for wildlife and people, restoring the carriers to their natural form and function, removing artificial structures, reshaping the riverbank, refreshing gravel beds and restoring bankside vegetation. As a result, numbers of wild fish species such as wild brown trout and grayling have increased allowing the development of a wild (non-stocked) fishery.

Restoration of marine habitats

Many people consider the seas around Britain to be cold, polluted and largely devoid of wildlife.[80] Yet, our seas retain a huge diversity of life. In places, the seabed is composed of rocky reefs covered in a faunal turf of soft corals, brittle stars, mussels and oysters. Forests of kelp are home to crustaceans and fish whilst our seas still support substantial commercial fisheries for cod, haddock, crab and lobster, for example. However, at the beginning of the nineteenth century, the seas were far more productive, with fisherman regularly catching more big fish with far less effort than today. For example, over 20,000 tonnes of common skate were landed each year during the 1920s; today this species is commercially extinct. Whitby was host to a major sport fishery for blue-fin tuna, a species that is almost absent from the North Sea today.

This vast diminution of marine wildlife has been driven above all by industrial fishing, and especially beam trawling that has destroyed the encrusting reefs converting them to shifting sands, muds and gravels.

In some ways, though, restoring the wildlife of the marine environment is much easier to achieve than on land. The diversity of life is largely intact, as there are only a few locally extinct or missing species, and that habitat by its very nature is highly connected. Where conservation measures are taken, restoration is remarkably rapid (see Case Study 24). The Wildlife Trusts' view is that the Government should set up regional seas plans that set out a spatial approach to restoration.[81] These plans should include: sustainable fishing areas – fishing within environmental limits and avoiding sensitive wildlife; resource areas of low environmental risk where development (for example, offshore wind farms) might be suitable; and, most crucially of all, wildlife areas – a network of marine protected areas that are managed as a whole to allow the recovery of marine wildlife.

───

Case Study 24 **Lamlash Bay**

The Firth of Clyde was once an important British fishery sustaining, amongst others, fisheries for herring, cod, mackerel, whiting, haddock, turbot and skate. After a century of overfishing, all these fish stocks collapsed. Marine habitats in the Firth are now ecologically simplified, composed mostly of mobile mud supporting only Nethrops (scampi-prawns) in commercially fishable quantities. As a result, the fishing communities that surround the Firth have largely gone.

In an effort to revive the wildlife of the Firth of Clyde, and in turn those coastal communities that depended on this wildlife, the Community of the Arran Seabed Trust (COAST) campaigned for Scotland's first marine 'no-take zone'. This marine protected area was set up in Lamlash Bay on the Isle of Arran in September 2008. Lamlash Bay's recovery has been rapid. Surveys were undertaken in 2010. Repeat surveys, after only three years in 2013, revealed 50% more scallops, twice as many encrusting organisms such as maerl, seaweeds, hydroids, bryozoans and sponges and an increase in adult lobster size. These surveys show that the structural diversity of the seabed, which has increased by 40% and in turn supports spawning and a restoration of fish in the Firth, can return and return rapidly if protected well.

Scottish Natural Heritage extended the tiny 1km² Lamlash Bay 'no-take zone' into a much bigger 250km² South Arran nature conservation marine protected area, designated in 2016.
It remains to be seen whether management measures proposed

by Scottish Natural Heritage and the enforcement required to regulate activity within the marine protected area will enable a wider recovery of the Firth of Forth.

—

Habitat creation

On land, the level of habitat destruction in the UK is remarkable. For example, of the 6.7 million hectares of neutral lowland hay meadow that existed just after the Second World War, only 150,000ha survive today – just 2.2%.[82] Likewise, 80% of Britain's lowland heaths have been lost since 1800.[83] Of the very best sites for nature conservation, identified by Charles Rothschild through the Society for the Promotion of Nature Reserves – the forerunner of The Wildlife Trusts (see Chapter 1), 30% have now been partially or entirely destroyed.[84]

As a result, to develop the ecological network recommended by Lawton et al., new habitat needs to be created. Some habitats simply cannot be created in any meaningful timescale. New woodlands, though wonderful for recreation and good for many generalist woodland species, cannot recreate ancient woodlands. Likewise, it is not possible to recreate peatland habitats as the process of peat formation takes many thousands of years.

Yet, for some habitats, creation can be quick and remarkably successful. For example, freshwater reedbeds were a very common habitat in the medieval period. Eastern England in particular had a dense network of freshwater, brackish and saltwater marshes that were often dominated by reed. The reedbeds supported a rich diversity of species including bittern, marsh harrier and bearded tit. However, land drainage and reedbed loss led to the extinction of bittern as a British breeding species by 1885 though the bird started breeding again in the early 1900s, reaching a high point of 50 booming males (i.e. breeding males) in the 1950s before declining again to just 11 booming males in 1997. Sustained action, especially by the RSPB, has turned the fortunes for bittern and today there are 164 booming males. At the heart of this success story is the creation of reedbed habitat (see Case Study 25).

Reedbed creation at Lakenheath

Before 1995, Lakenheath was typical of the Suffolk countryside – intensively farmed arable land. Since the purchase of the land by the RSPB, 300ha of new grazing marsh and reedbed have been created. Over 2km of ditches were reshaped with shallow sloping sides to encourage reed growth and to provide feeding areas that are particularly suitable for bittern. Water levels are controlled by sluices allowing the RSPB to manage the reedbeds at an optimal depth for bittern and to drain down the reedbeds for cutting, so as to avoid the beds becoming dominated by willow. The results have been remarkable, with fenland wildlife returning to the site in abundance including such rarities as common crane (that are now far from common in Britain), marsh harriers and a record of eight booming male bitterns in 2017.

→
Lakenheath Fen.

Within the minerals industry, mitigation for actual or potential habitat destruction has been used to create new habitats after mining has ceased. The RSPB analysed existing mineral sites in the UK showing that they covered 64,000ha and assessing that about 55,000ha could contribute to meeting the UK's BAP commitments by helping to creating 17 different types of priority habitat.[85] A good example of this approach is Yorkshire Wildlife Trust's North Cave Wetlands Reserve (see Case Study 26). Similarly, in the coalfields of the UK, deep and opencast mining have also led to the creation of new nature areas. Case Study 27 sets out three examples in the Yorkshire coalfield of this approach. In the first, subsidence resulting from deep mining of coal led to the development of Potteric Carr Nature Reserve near Doncaster. In the second, opencast mining was the precursor to the new wetlands at St Aidens on the edge of Leeds, whilst the third is a good example of how post-industrial sites (in this case also from coal mining) can be redeveloped for wildlife and recreation.

Case Study 26   **North Cave Wetlands**

To the west of Hull, late glacial fluvial gravels were mined by a local company, Humberstone Aggregates, creating a hole which was destined for use as a landfill site. Opposition to landfill by local residents eventually led to the 'hole' being bought by a local resident and donated to the Yorkshire Wildlife Trust to manage as a nature reserve. With help and support from Humberstone Aggregates, the slopes were shallowed and weirs used to create a nature reserve. The reserve is now rich in wildlife, with over 200 bird species recorded on the site. The original nature reserve is expanding through two further planning applications for mineral extraction. For these planning applications, Humberstone Aggregates worked alongside Yorkshire Wildlife Trust for planning permission to develop a nature reserve through mineral extraction, developing a Section 106 legal agreement alongside the planning application to pass on the freehold of the mineral site and an endowment for future management of the reserve. Local opposition was minimal. In summer, thousands of birdwatchers come to North Cave to witness at close hand breeding avocet amongst a welter of

→
Sand and gravel extraction next to North Cave Wetlands. Restoration of these workings will be used to extend the existing reserve westwards.

71

other wildlife. The site includes footpaths, a cafe, hides and other viewing areas. An innovation has been developing hides in the middle of gravel workings, allowing visitors to watch the transformation of gravel pit to nature reserve.

Recreating habitat in the Yorkshire coalfield

Potteric Carr Nature Reserve

The land to the east of Doncaster is low lying, flat and sits at about sea level. It was once glacial Lake Humber – a huge lake that sat behind ice that dammed its exit into what is now the North Sea Basin (and then a land bridge to continental Europe dominated by the River Rhine floodplain that joined the Thames to the south). When the ice melted and sea levels rose, the bed of glacial Lake Humber became the northern part of the vast East of England fenland stretching from Cambridge to the edge of York. In the 1700s, this land was drained following the work of the Dutch drainage engineer Vermuyden. Rivers were straightened and run above the land surface enclosed in embankments. The land could then be drained through a network of ditches that fed into lower-lying drains that were eventually pumped into the rivers. This allowed landowners to enclose the common-land wetlands into privately owned farmland. At Doncaster, land drainage also allowed the development of coal mines in this drained landscape with, for example, Rossington Pit developing on what was once wet fenland.

In turn, a few kilometres to the south-east of Doncaster, deep mining of coal led to land adjacent to the main Edinburgh to London railway to subside. The resulting depression at Low Ellers Carr filled with water, with wetland plants rapidly recolonising the lake; a fragment of the lost fenland landscape returned to Doncaster. By the 1960s, this site had become well known to birdwatchers who under the aegis of Yorkshire Wildlife Trust (who took a lease on this site) formed a group to manage the new Low Ellers Carr Nature Reserve. Over the next 40 years, Roger Mitchell and his volunteers oversaw a massive expansion of the reserve, creating new wetland habitats to clean urban street water from the main drain across the site and to act as flood storage for new developments. As Doncaster has expanded, urban development threatened to cut off the reserve from the wider countryside leading to Yorkshire Wildlife Trust buying agricultural land, excavating topsoil and creating more wetland habitat. The resulting Potteric Carr Nature Reserve is now so big, fenland specialists such as marsh harrier and bittern have returned as breeding birds to the site.

→
Map of
Potteric Carr
Nature Reserve.

→
Marsh harrier
chicks at
Potteric Carr
Nature Reserve.

St Aidan's Nature Reserve

To the east of Leeds, where the coal runs closer to the surface, deep mining was replaced by opencast coal mining. Opencasting is, of course, enormously destructive and decimates the original landscape. That does, however, leave a 'blank canvas' for habitat creation and often a canvas full of mined out depressions that naturally fill with water. The RSPB, working alongside Leeds City Council, Harworth Estates and UK Coal, used this opportunity to create a series of shallow lagoons, reedbeds and grazing marsh along the Lower Aire Valley. The site now forms the newly created (it formally opened in 2017) St Aidan's Nature Reserve. This reserve now fits into a mosaic of new habitats that have been created as a result of deindustrialisation.

Rothwell Country Park

To the east of St Aidan's are mining subsidence lagoons (also RSPB reserves) at Fairburn Ings. To the west, slag (coal spoil from deep mines) heaps have been restored into meadows and new woodlands. For example, Rothwell Country Park (now a Leeds City Council and Yorkshire Wildlife Trust Nature Reserve) is a mosaic of woodland, meadow and pond on the site of the former Rothwell Colliery. The colliery, one of the oldest in the Leeds area, shut in 1983 after 116 years of operation. The mining village of Rothwell suffered greatly with the impact of unemployment after the mine shut. Today, Rothwell is on the up partly because of regeneration of the former colliery site as a nature reserve and it is now a pleasant commuter village serving Leeds.

Taken together, the network of restored slag heaps, mining subsidence lagoons and St Aidan's itself form a remarkable ecological network stretching along the Lower Aire valley. With the high-speed HS2 railway line set to cut through the Lower Aire Valley it will be important for planners to work closely with HS2 Ltd to ensure the line enhances rather than destroys this ecological network.

A very different type of habitat creation is now required along the east and southern coasts of Britain. In glacial times, the north-west of Britain was weighed down by up to a kilometre of ice.[86] The weight of this ice was so great it depressed the continental plate causing the north-west to sink and the south-east of the UK to rise. Once the ice melted, the plate sprung back though the action is extremely slow, taking place over many thousands of years. Such isostatic change is exhibited in Scotland through the development of coastal raised wave-cut platforms. These flat benches of land sit above the existing beach composed of beach sands and shingle formed when the land was lower relative to sea level. For example, the village of Ullapool sits on an extensive raised beach on Loch Broom. The opposite effect is found in the south-east, where the land is slowly sinking back. In combination with a rising sea level, driven by a warming and thermally expanding ocean,[87] relative sea level is rising fast. In east Yorkshire, for example, the soft cliffs of Holderness are eroding rapidly with a seaward advance of metres each year. The impact is profound with lost villages, roads falling into the sea and wartime sea defences collapsing onto the beach.

→
Road collapse
on the
Holderness
Coast,
East Yorkshire.

→
Managed
realignment at
Paull Holme
Strays.

Moreover, where farmland has been formed by embanking shallow coastal tidal marshes, sea defences are becoming increasingly inadequate and expensive to maintain. Cost–benefit analyses are undertaken to assess the sense in maintaining these defences and, in places, it is clear that there is no economic rationale for the State to continue to maintain the defences; it is cheaper to return land to the sea – a managed realignment of the coast (see Case Study 28). In a similar vein, where a rising sea level comes up against a hard sea defence, European designated (as SPAs or SACs) coastal marshes are squeezed between the rising sea and the hard flood defence, requiring statutory authorities (usually the Environment Agency) to recreate these habitats elsewhere. The most cost-effective way to achieve this is to breach sea walls and allow seawater to restore salt marshes and mudflats along the coast – another example of managed realignment. Page 75 shows an example of managed realignment at Paull Holme Strays in East Yorkshire. Here, new sea walls have been built at the back of the site to allow a breach in the sea walls at the front thus flooding farmland to create new salt marshes and mudflats as mitigation for habitat losses from development and coastal squeeze.

Another reason to realign the coast is to reduce coastal flooding. This can be achieved by allowing more spreading room for high water or by creating new salt marshes. At Alkborough in North Lincolnshire a managed realignment of the upper Humber estuary was achieved by breaching sea embankments. Farmland is now flooded at high tide creating new salt marshes. Alkborough lies at the landward end of the funnel-like Humber estuary allowing very high tide flows or storm surges to spread across the salt marsh rather than funnel up the estuary causing overtopping of sea defences and flooding of land and buildings. In the December 2013 storm surge, modelling suggested that habitat recreation at Alkborough lowered upper Humber storm surge levels substantially reducing coastal flooding. This storm surge breached sea defences further down the Humber at Welwick. Fortunately, the flood embankments at Welwick are fronted by a substantial area of salt marsh that takes the energy out of storm surge waves as they run across the marshes.[88] It is very likely that without such salt marsh, the breach would have been far worse with far greater coastal flooding.

___

Case Study 28 **Managed realignment at Abbotts Hall Farm**

Abbotts Hall Farm is adjacent to the Blackwater Estuary in Essex. On the seaward side, land had been protected from inundation for hundreds of years through a sea wall. Cost–benefit analyses could not justify continued maintenance of the sea wall whilst rising sea levels meant that salt marsh was being lost through 'coastal squeeze'. As a result, Essex Wildlife Trust bought the farm (it is now their headquarters) and, with funding from World Wide Fund for Nature and the Heritage Lottery Fund, planned a managed realignment of the coast with the statutory agencies. This was one of the first realignments in the UK and securing planning permission proved very difficult. In particular, objections were raised by local oyster fishermen who were concerned that the alignment might cause silting in the oyster beds, and the RSPB who were concerned about impacts on coastal erosion on the opposite bank of the Blackwater. Modelling showed that the impact would be minor in both cases. In addition, the site had great crested newts, sitting within a SPA and SSSI which made planning for realignment difficult.

Once permission was secured, the land was reshaped through the construction of spur walls, to protect neighbouring farmland, and feeder creeks to promote salt marsh formation in what had been arable fields. Freshwater ponds were developed to allow great crested newt relocation. The wall was breached in 2002, opening up about 80ha of land that has now developed into salt marshes and mudflats.

Rewilding

All the case studies above seek to maintain, enhance or create particular outcomes. At Wheldrake Ings, management is designed to maintain the flower-rich lowland meadows that have been in place for at least a thousand years; at Lakenheath, the objective is to create wetland habitats and in particular reedbeds; at Abbotts Hall Farm, managed realignment is designed to create salt marsh. The starting point for all these endeavours is to achieve the desired outcome.

In an era of rapidly changing climate, this approach may not work anymore. Everywhere in the landscape of the British Isles is a record of the impact of global cooling. Only 15,000 years ago, ice stretched from the poles down the North Sea basin to Norfolk, through the Vale of Mowbray to York and across Wales to the north coast of Devon. To the south of the ice sheets, the English landscape was akin to the tundra of Siberia. Yet, such global cooling amounted to only perhaps 9°C at its height.[89] Human-influenced global warming is likely to be in the order of 4–5°C. In a similar fashion, albeit with very different results to the dramatic impacts of recent global cooling, global warming will have a profound impact on the environment of Britain, with southern England having a climate more akin to southern Europe today.

At Wheldrake Ings (see Case Study 20), for example, managers agonised over how quickly to let water off the Ings in spring (controlled by a weir) and the precise height at which water should be held over the winter and early spring. These arguments continued until it was pointed out that current climate variability, which is increasing as a result of climate change, is greater than any changes to the water management regime proposed and will be dwarfed by even greater variability as climate change takes hold – all of which is unpredictable as yet.

Accordingly, many conservationists are moving away from an outcome-based management paradigm to one where the outcome is a process rather than a fixed objective. Indeed, some argue that conservation should direct itself towards the restoration of natural processes regardless of the eventual habitat and species outcome that might ensue. Monbiot sets this out rather captivatingly in his book *Feral*, coining the term 'rewilding'. He captures the approach, saying:

> Rewilding, unlike conservation, has no fixed objective: it is driven not by human management but by natural processes. Rewilding . . . does not seek . . . to control the natural world, to recreate a particular ecosystem or landscape . . . The process is the outcome.[90]

This very different approach in which the goal is to restore trophic diversity, i.e. to enhance the opportunities for animals and plants to feed on each other, is about restoring the web of life that supports rich ecosystems. Such trophic diversity is highly diminished in Britain. Many top predators – bears, wolves, wolverines and lynx – have been hunted to extinction. Habitats have been substantially simplified in ecological terms, especially as a result of intensive agriculture. The sheep-shorn uplands are particularly picked out by Monbiot as lacking in trophic diversity; an arable field, where every 'weed' is killed by herbicide and the soil fauna impoverished through regular doses of fertiliser and pesticide, is of course in far poorer ecological condition.

The approach gives prominence to keystone species – those species that play a substantial role in the development of the environment. Sphagnum moss, for example, is the keystone species for Britain's peatlands, having turned lowland fens into raised bogs and Britain's wetter uplands and western areas into blanket bog; 9% of Britain has been dramatically altered by sphagnum moss. Another example is the reintroduction of wolves in Yellowstone, in North America, that caused a dramatic change to the ecology of the whole park by reducing deer numbers and changing their feeding habits. Beaver dams serve to create new wetlands, filter out silt from rivers and reduce storm flows, reducing flooding downstream. One of the cheapest ways to reduce urban flooding in Britain would be to reintroduce beavers (or simply allow them to spread from the toehold they now have in Scotland and Devon).

A Dutch ecologist, Frans Vera, believes that the dense, closed-canopy 'wildwood' that existed before Neolithic agriculture was actually rather open, more a parkland landscape than closed-canopy forest; the result of large herds of grazing animals – keystone species – in particular horse, deer and aurochs (extinct pre-domesticated cattle).[91] These concepts have been tested at Oostvaardersplassen in the Netherlands (see Case Study 29).

Few people argue that we should entirely abandon rare habitats and species assemblages to the fate of rewilding. In our fragmented lowlands, places of particular note, with interesting assemblages of species, should continue to be managed for that assemblage, though even here there is room for rewilding (see Case Study 30). Likewise, there needs to be space to conserve some of our cherished cultural landscape – coppiced woodlands, meadows and heathlands, for example. However, for less populated parts of Britain – the uplands, the Highlands of Scotland or the wilder stretches of coast and river – rewilding could well be the key to the restoration of Britain's wildlife and all the services that flow from that.

Oostvaardersplassen – Rewilding the polders

Oostvaardersplassen is a polder, reclaimed from the North Sea in 1968, which initially developed a range of habitats to the extent that by 1989 it had achieved international importance as a wetland. Since then, it has been seen by ecologists as an experiment in rewilding, although not entirely without management. It is a large area comprising 3,500ha of wetland and 2,000ha of dry grazing habitat. The wetland areas support a variety of bird species including white-tailed eagles and bittern. The dry grassland habitat is maintained by introducing grazing animals such as Konik ponies, a wild horse species from Eastern Europe, and Heck cattle, a breed close to the auroch, an extinct species of cattle which grazed European grasslands in prehistory, as well as red deer. Whilst it is recognised as an example of rewilding, the herds of cattle actually have to be culled, otherwise in the absence of large predators they would destroy the habitat through overgrazing and die of starvation.

→
Geese
flying over
Oostvaarder-
splassen Nature
Reserve,
Netherlands.

The Knepp Estate

In 1978, Charles Burrell inherited the Knepp Estate and fully expected to carry on its farming traditions. However, the heavy clay soils of the Weald make for difficult agriculture and, despite modernisation under the Burrells, the farm was rarely profitable leading to a decision to sell the dairy herds and put the arable out to contract in 2000. At the same time, the family turned their attention to restoring Repton Park around the castle. This included introducing fallow deer and reinstating flower-rich meadows. The approach was transformational with wildlife – butterflies, bees and birds – returning in rich profusion

Emboldened by this transformation, the Burrells decided to dispense with loss-making arable agriculture entirely in 2002 and move towards a very different process-led non-goal-oriented approach that worked with rather than against nature. Charles Burrell was keen to explore the ideas of Frans Vera allowing two ecological processes to operate – trampling and grazing working sometimes in opposition to vegetation succession. Longhorn cattle, Exmoor ponies, Tamworth pigs, and fallow, red and roe deer were introduced into 2,500 acres of former arable land and allowed to run wild. In the absence of any natural predators, culling takes place with the Estate selling about 75 tonnes of live-weight meat per year. Effectively, the Burrells have introduced a form of very low (economic) input and low-intensity farming that can make money and allows ecological processes (rewilding) free reign.

The results of this experiment have been phenomenal. Fast declining and extremely rare wildlife such as nightingale, turtle dove and purple emperor butterflies have all now returned to the estate in large numbers.

The Knepp Estate itself has developed a visitor economy through its associated tourist activities, with visitors coming to what is now a gorgeous wildlife-rich landscape in the heart of intensively farmed southern England. This experiment shows what is possible on the more marginal soils of Britain, demonstrating that profitable land use is possible by drastically reducing agricultural intensity and allowing rewilding rather than continuing with intensive Government (tax-payer) subsidy-driven agriculture.

––

Conclusions

Rewilding challenges the whole nature conservation paradigm that has been based on the conservation of particular habitats and species and in turn the conservation of a series of places that exhibit those habitats or species. A site-based approach to conservation, with fixed habitat or species outcomes, has clearly not worked – Britain's wildlife continues to decline and with it a range of essential ecosystem services such as flood prevention, pollution amelioration, pollination of food crops and soil for food growing. Indeed, an increasing body of literature shows that the diminution of wildlife and an increasing disconnection between people and the natural world also diminishes human health and happiness.

A different approach is required. Land use and marine planning should move far beyond the planning of hard infrastructure towards an explicit (i.e. spatially recognised) ecological network approach. This would include the management of places for particular habitats and species and, increasingly, simply restoring as much diversity as possible to allow natural processes to take hold.

Chapter 5

Rewilding the City

Introduction

Reintroducing nature into cities is not a new idea – from the urban parks created by civic benefactors in the nineteenth century to the garden city movement, open space and access to nature has been a component of urban design and management for the past century and a half. In this chapter, we trace the origins of urban greening and the growing recognition that towns and cities have a major role to play in nature conservation as habitats disappear and are fragmented in the countryside through development and agricultural intensification. It explores initiatives such as urban and community forests pioneered in the Netherlands and the urban wildlife movement which gathered momentum in Europe during the later years of the last century.

This chapter also considers the benefits to urban communities of having access to nature and the many other ecosystem services that nature provides for cities. The positive impact of nature on human health and psychological well-being is a central theme in urban rewilding as well as engaging communities in the appreciation and ideally management of their local environments. The concept of re-naturing at the metropolitan scale has been a recent focus of UN and EU programmes and policy.[92]

Finally, we consider urban design and management measures which can encourage wildlife in towns and cities – green roofs, sustainable urban drainage schemes, ecological management of public green space and gardens, for example.

Interest in parks and open space in cities has a long history – nineteenth-century struggles to save Hampstead Heath, developing urban parks in the newly created Victorian cities of England and garden cities in the early twentieth century, for example. Behind this interest was not so much the preservation of wildlife, rather the benefits of public access to green spaces and improved living conditions for citizens. These green spaces were thought of as a reconnection of urban populations with the natural environment through a combination of city and countryside.[93] Equally, the many natural history societies that were established in the nineteenth century were mainly concerned with recording species of animals and plants rather than actively conserving nature. From both these perspectives, urban areas were often considered devoid of wildlife interest and public parks, although providing green space, were often planted with exotic species of plants collected from around the world and displayed in formal bedding schemes.

A more holistic approach to urban ecology has gathered strength since the millennium, labelled as 'nature-based solutions'. It is based on the ecosystem services provided by the natural environment and more natural urban design. Scott and Lennon describe this as:

> Nature-based solutions applied at the urban scale emphasise multifunctionality in terms of services and functions to include drainage management, habitat provision, ecological connectivity, health and well-being, recreational space, energy reduction and climate change, mitigation and adaptation. This suggests a range of scalar interventions, from the design of city-wide ecological networks to local multifunctional urban parks providing recreational functions and cooling/flood alleviation services, and micro-scale design including streetscapes designed to retain water (e.g. rain gardens, roadside bioswales) and the integration of living systems with built systems such as green walls and green roofs to reduce heat stress.[94]

The European Commission has recently funded a programme addressing nature-based solutions to urban problems.[95] Four key themes were identified:

- **Enhancing sustainable urbanisation:** use of natural areas and features in and around cities to perform essential ecosystem services – adaptation to climate change, increased resilience to drought, flooding and high temperatures, and social health and happiness.
- **Restoring degraded ecosystems:** restoring natural vegetation to provide services such as water purification, flood damage control and recreational opportunities.
- **Developing climate change adaptation and resilience:** using nature-based solutions to provide more resilient responses and enhance the storage of carbon.
- **Improving risk management and resilience:** implementing nature-based solutions to offer major opportunities to reduce the frequency and/or intensity of different types of hazards. Therefore, they should form part of a range of measures and actions in integrated risk management, as they can provide more advantages than conventional methods. They combine multiple functions and benefits, for example pollution reduction, carbon storage, biodiversity conservation and the provision of recreational activities and economic opportunities.

This theme of 'nature-based solutions' encapsulates the range of issues considered here, largely focusing on ecosystem services approaches to urban development and management including natural landscaping, the role of nature in improving public health and happiness, ecological approaches to building design and estate layout, sustainable urban drainage and water quality, and green infrastructure. Damage, disturbance and measures to reduce the impact of activities such as dog walking and predation by domestic pets, are also considered.

Natural landscaping
The creation of more natural landscapes in cities was pioneered in the Netherlands where the Amsterdam Bos (Forest), established during the 1930s, was designed to replicate the types of vegetation naturally occurring in the Dutch polder lands.

The enlightened city council considered, that natural landscaping would require much less maintenance than traditional urban parks with their exotic planting schemes and intensive grassland management. In the years following the Second World War, the Dutch developed this naturalistic style, creating wild landscapes in the new suburbs called 'heeme' or home parks – planted with native species. Similar early examples of natural landscaping are found in Norway and Sweden. These ideas gained greater following during the late 1960s and 1970s and were used, for example, in the design of Warrington New Town in the UK, although the management of many parks and green spaces continued to feature colourful introduced plants in densely planted formally laid out borders and closely mown grass lawns. Pressure for change built during the 1980s with growth of urban wildlife movements in the large conurbations, for example LWT and the Urban Wildlife Group in the West Midlands. Examples of alternative approaches using seeding of wildflowers to create meadows rather than closely mown lawns are now becoming more common. The Sheffield Green Estate social enterprise, for example, initially seeded some 300ha of land where houses had been demolished. Whilst only temporary, this treatment nevertheless transformed once no-go areas. This approach was rolled out to other green spaces in the city and has been adopted elsewhere, for example, on roadside verges and central reservations on dual carriageways (see Case Study 31).

Case Study 31   **Naturalistic roadside planting in Sheffield**

A partnership between Streets Ahead, which manages green spaces in the city, University of Sheffield and Sheffield & Rotherham Wildlife Trust, as part of the Living Highways project, is transforming roadside verges and roundabouts into wildflower meadows. The cutting regimes have been reduced on some verges to allow wildflowers to set seed. This approach should benefit biodiversity in the city as well as potentially reducing flood risk and improving air quality. The partnership is working on 28 sites across the city with a focus on changing mowing frequency. Trial sites have ranged from broad open road verges such as on Bochum Parkway to small patches of grass in residential areas.

Naturalistic
roadside
planting,
Sheffield.

The University is evaluating how the change in mowing
frequency impacts on biodiversity as well as what the public
think about the changes. Early signs are positive. At Bochum
Parkway, for example, orchids are flourishing. The intention is
eventually to roll out this approach across the whole city.

With the growing interest in urban wildlife, many new wildlife
areas were created on post-industrial and other derelict land.
Camley Street in London, close to King's Cross and St Pancras
railway stations, is a good example of new habitat created on old
industrial land, rescued from its intended use as a lorry park (see
Case Study 33). There was also a growing awareness of the
conservation needs of those relics of disappearing countryside
habitat such as commons and churchyards. In Greater London,
for example, there are many natural green spaces including some
2,500ha of ancient woodland. Many other large cities are similarly
endowed with green space and wildlife. Forty percent of the area
of Stockholm, for example, consists of green space whilst
Singapore, a densely packed island city of five million people, still
includes ten different ecosystems types.[96] UK examples of urban
nature reserves that still contain the 'relict' native flora of the
city's rural past include the Avon Gorge in Bristol, Ken Wood in
Hampstead, London, and the core of Holyrood Park in Edinburgh.

←
High species
diversity on a
brownfield site
in Barnsley.

←
Low species
diversity on an
arable field.

Many post-industrial development (brownfield) sites have
been colonised naturally, providing unusual wildlife interest in
places. For example, extensive steel works waste tips in North
East England, South Yorkshire and South Wales often support
communities of lime-loving plants that contrast sharply to the
habitats around them. The banks of the River Don in Sheffield
have been colonised by fig trees from seeds washed down from
human sewage and germinated as a result of the once-higher
water temperature of the river, heated by the factories
surrounding it. Indeed, brownfield sites can be very rich in
biodiversity, creating a dilemma for planners who would normally
see previously developed brownfield land as opportunities for
new development, with local communities often asking for such
sites to be 'tidied up'. The richness of brownfield sites can be
appreciated by comparing a typically intensive arable field to a

typically biodiverse brownfield site (see opposite). As the figure shows, brownfield sites can often support a wide range of wild plant (and invertebrate) species, some of which colonised naturally, and others perhaps sown as part of a land reclamation scheme. In addition to their wildlife interest, brownfield sites can also provide access to nature in some of the most deprived urban neighbourhoods.

Tree planting has been a popular response to environmental improvement in urban areas and many millions of trees have been planted in the UK in a variety of programmes from 'plant a tree in [nineteen] seventy-three' to the Community Forest Programme begun in the 1990s and still active in some parts (although the official programme ended in 2005). As part of the Community Forest Programme, many new plantation woodlands were created in urban fringe areas, using mainly native species of trees in naturalistic planting schemes inspired by Dutch practice. An evaluation of the programme indicates that it successively met targets for woodland creation, non-woodland habitat creation and creation/restoration of hedgerows. Some 10,000ha of new woodland was planted, together with 1,200km of new or restored hedgerow and 12,000ha of other habitats.[97] However, the wildlife benefits of many of these tree-planting programmes remain to be realised and despite planting mainly native tree species, many of the young trees were sourced from outside the UK. To avoid the

→
Volunteers
planting trees
at Newbiggin
Nature Reserve,
Craven,
Yorkshire.

spread of disease and maintain local genetic material, future planting schemes should ideally use locally sourced planting stock and seeds. An alternative approach would be to allow more natural regeneration of woodland. However they were established, ongoing management of the new woodlands has been an issue in some areas, although the evaluation report also points to ongoing social and health benefits, noting that the 'contribution to the public health agenda is an important wider outcome. Through forging links with Primary Care Trusts and Mental Health Care Trusts, a number of community forests are helping to address physical and mental health issues.'[98]

The design of Queen Elizabeth Olympic Park in London, site of the 2012 Olympic and Paralympic Games, took on board the principles of naturalistic planting as part of its approach to sustainable urbanisation. This allowed nature-based solutions to waste water treatment and building design to be incorporated into the design of the Olympic arenas (see Case Study 32).

Case Study 32   **Queen Elizabeth Olympic Park**

A commitment to sustainability was made at the beginning of design work for the Queen Elizabeth Olympic Park. The aim was to construct sustainable buildings, water networks and waste water treatment; natural parkland solutions to flood risk and management; restoration of canals and brownfield land; a network of sustainable transport facilities; and engender a changed mindset in the construction and service industries. The site was also to provide a legacy of sporting and other

→
Naturalistic planting at Queen Elizabeth Olympic Park, London.

recreational facilities, natural parkland alongside clean rivers and well-designed housing for local people. Landscaping of the Olympic Park created wildlife and recreational corridors linking the River Thames with open countryside via the Lee Valley Regional Park.

On completion of the Olympic and Paralympic Games, the London Legacy Development Corporation (LLDC) has taken responsibility for the park and its future development is set out in the Legacy Communities Scheme (LCS). The Scheme provides for the creation of new neighbourhoods and a business zone, and enhancing biodiversity is a key part of this development. 'Biodiversity plays a key role in achieving all of this, as our natural environment underpins our health, wellbeing, and economic prosperity. Enhancing biodiversity of the Park and within the LCS is therefore one of our top priorities.'[99] BAP, which was required as part of the outline planning permission, sets out the objectives:

- Set out a Park wide quantum of BAP habitat of 49.1ha

- Build on and deliver the vision for biodiversity enhancement and conservation in the Park and identify strategic directions that take account of the international, national, regional, and local conservation scene

- Provide a guide to nature conservation measures and biodiversity objectives for all those involved in the management and maintenance of the Park

- Outline actions required to establish and conserve species and habitats of conservation concern in the Park

- Set out the detailed maintenance and management regime for BAP habitat in the Park

- Outline long-term management actions to ensure successful establishment and an increase in value of created habitat

- Promote co-ordinated action and increased effort to benefit wildlife in the Park

- Provide opportunities for local people to get involved in nature conservation work and biodiversity related activities.[100]

New habitats to be created include species-rich grasslands, trees and scrub, wet woodland, reedbed and ponds. LLDC has committed to undertaking Annual Biodiversity Monitoring

Reports detailing the surveys undertaken and their findings, with year-on-year comparisons and comparisons with the original BAP 2008 monitoring data. Progress towards BAP biodiversity targets will be assessed and recommendations made for improving biodiversity work.

The commercial property sector is also becoming more actively involved in urban greening initiatives. In London, some of the biggest property development companies (Crown Estates, Grosvenor Britain and Ireland, Shaftsbury, Howard de Walden and the Portman Estate) are investing in the Wild West End project. The objective is to create corridors and stepping stones linking the major open spaces and parks together. The first stage, an ecological masterplan for St James's and Regent Street, will link Regent's Park with St James's Park, using features such as green walls and roofs, natural planting schemes, bird and bat boxes.

Nature and well-being

A constant cross-cutting theme in urban nature-based policy is that access to nature is good for human well-being and as such it can improve health and reduce the escalating costs of medical treatment. There is a wealth of evidence on the positive effect that spending time in the natural environment has on the health and emotional well-being of children and it is recognised that the quality of the local natural environment is one of the factors that shapes all our health over a lifetime.[101] A good environment is associated with a decrease in problems such as high blood pressure, high cholesterol, obesity and depression. It is also linked with better mental health, reduced stress and more physical activity. Moreover, access to nature and green space has been shown to improve people's perceived happiness. In England, the benefits of urban green spaces for physical and mental health have been estimated to reduce treatment costs by £2.1 billion.[102]

An academic study of participants in The Wildlife Trusts' 30 Days Wild programme, which aims to get people to do something in the natural environment every day for the month of June, found a strong association between participation and perceived increases in health and happiness.

→
30 Days Wild is
an initiative to
connect people
to their natural
environment.

The . . . analysis suggests that the improvement in
reported general health was related to the improvement
in happiness, mediated by the increase in nature
connection. Links between nature connection and
happiness have been established previously but
understanding the link to health is of value. Our findings
suggest that connection to nature may provide people
with resilience to meet the challenges of everyday life,
while also facilitating exercise, social contact and
a sense of purpose.[103]

Involvement in practical work to enhance wildlife has been
shown to have a positive impact on health and well-being in
research looking at volunteering on nature reserves. It found that:

The percentage of participants reporting low wellbeing
scores (defined by UK norms) declined from 39% at
baseline to only 19% at 12-weeks. Indeed, to a
statistically significant extent, the positive impact on
mental wellbeing was greater for individuals with low
wellbeing to start with (compared to individuals who

had average to high wellbeing to start with). 95% of participants with low wellbeing at baseline reported an improvement at 6-weeks, and for the baseline to 12-weeks sample, this figure was 83%. Participants also reported statistically significant enhanced levels of health, positivity, nature relatedness, pro-environmental behaviour and physical activity, and increased frequency of contact with greenspaces.[104]

→
Volunteers
erecting
bat boxes.

→
Volunteers
improving
their local
environment
at Woodberry
Wetlands,
London.

Urban nature reserves such as Camley Street, in the heart of London, provide outlets for local people to engage with nature and for them to become actively engaged as volunteers (see Case Study 33). The involvement of local people not just as users but also in the active enhancement and maintenance of their green spaces is a key objective of urban conservation. Successful examples of engaging local people in managing and improving their local environments are Natural Estates, a partnership to improve green spaces on housing estates in London, and My Wild City in Bristol (see Case Studles 34 and 35).

Case Study 33 **Camley Street Natural Park**

The site, a former coal yard in central London, nestles between two of the city's busiest railway stations, King's Cross and St Pancras, and adjoins the Regent's Canal. It fell out of use in 1970 and the then local authority planned to develop it as a lorry park. A successful campaign, run by the nascent LWT and local people, saved the flower-rich wasteland from development and its management was taken on by LWT in 1984; it was opened in 1985 and became a Local Nature Reserve in 1986. It is well used by local people and schools and is also a tourist attraction for overseas visitors.

Today the park sits at the heart of the King's Cross regeneration programme. While the landscape around it has transformed beyond recognition since the 1980s, it has continued to quietly provide a sanctuary for nature and a space for people to learn, volunteer or simply enjoy the tranquillity of their nature reserve; a butterfly's flight from St Pancras International Station. By 2020, 45,000 people will live, work and study within 1km of the park.

Whilst small (0.8ha), the woodland, grassland and wetland habitats, including ponds, reedbed and marshy areas, provide a rich habitat for birds, butterflies, amphibians and plant life, and a visitor centre caters for the thousands who visit annually. The centre is about to be replaced with a state-of-the-art ecologically sensitive building to provide a better facility to house staff, run volunteers and cater for Camley Street park's many visitors.

Case Study 34 **Natural Estates, London**

The aim of the project, which was funded through the Big Lottery in collaboration with Natural England, was to engage residents in enhancing and maintaining the biodiversity value of common green spaces. For the residents involved, there were benefits of improved physical and emotional health, better social cohesion and active citizenship. More than 7,000 residents took part from nine different housing estates.

Tasks undertaken included making balcony planters, hanging baskets, raised beds, bat boxes, minibeast shelters, hedgehog hibernacula, stag beetle loggeries and wildflower meadows. They also learnt about habitats and their management and how to carry out wildlife surveys, so that improvements were sustained beyond the life of the project.

Case Study 35

My Wild City

My Wild City in Bristol is a community engagement project that is transforming parts of the city. The vision is a city where whole streets get together to join up wildlife-friendly gardens and where communities and businesses are engaged in transforming and managing their local green spaces. For example, 30 households at Stanley Park in the city, who signed up to a wild-garden makeover with Avon Wildlife Trust, saw their front gardens transformed into a haven for nature and people. Stanley Park now provides a wildlife corridor between two neighbouring green spaces, allowing wildlife to move more easily.

→
My Wild Street,
Stanley Park,
Bristol.

Building design and estate layout

Given the scale of biodiversity loss and the degradation of ecosystem services, plans for new development projects should protect existing environmental capital and ideally should also enhance it wherever possible. Enhancing biodiversity in new development is best begun at the initial design stage rather than later, by which time efforts can sometimes only mitigate the impacts of development or compensate for losses of habitat and species. Requirements for the treatment of biodiversity in the design of development proposals are succinctly set out by Exeter City Council:

> The Design and Access Statement must set out the baseline ecological value of the site and proposals to enhance biodiversity. To do this a full ecological survey should be carried out by an appropriately qualified ecologist using recognised methodology. This should be followed by consideration by the ecologist and design team of the best way to retain and enhance existing ecological features (including links to off-site habitats and ecological features) and provide the opportunity for new habitats and increased biodiversity within the development.[105]

Measures to improve biodiversity should be explored throughout development schemes including within the fabric of the built development, and within the wider landscape and open space provision. The Wildlife Trusts identified 15 ways in which housing developments can benefit wildlife (see Case Study 36).

Case Study 36   **Wildlife design considerations**

- Permeable driveways to help reduce flood risk
- Trees, hedgerows, water and other habitats integrated with development
- Wildflower verges along roads and other formal open spaces
- Lighting designed to avoid disturbing wildlife
- Sustainable urban drainage, swales and rain gardens for wildlife and flood relief
- Bat roosts, bird boxes and other wildlife features designed into buildings
- Renewable energy and water efficiency built in from the outset

- Safe, attractive, connected pedestrian and cycle routes
- Features and corridors to help invertebrates, reptiles, hedgehogs and other mammals
- Wildlife friendly-green roofs and walls
- Native wildlife-friendly plants of local origin used in gardens and landscaping
- Wildlife-permeable boundaries between gardens and open space
- Allotments and community orchards for local food
- Street trees for wildlife, shade and improved air quality
- Interpretation panels to help people understand the needs of wildlife and the environment.[106]

Within the building fabric, appropriate measures include installation of bird and bat boxes, creation of roof voids and living roofs and walls which also reduce heat stress in buildings. Provision of artificial nest sites is useful because of the general lack of nesting opportunities in modern buildings which no longer provide gaps within the structure that nature previously took advantage of.

Opportunities within site landscaping include planting of hedgerows using species native to the area; wildlife-friendly tree and shrub planting; wildflower-rich grasslands; restoring the naturalness of water courses; maintaining a mosaic of grasslands and bare land with areas of long grass; and flower-rich meadows, all of which provide food, shelter and breeding places for wildlife. These features should be located to maximise linkages with nearby green spaces, habitats and wildlife corridors. Vegetation, whether forming roofs, walls or landscaping can mitigate the effects of high temperature in cities – they are clearly a great deal cooler when exposed to direct sun than concrete!

Guidance is also available on how to accommodate specific species of animals within the fabric of buildings, notably birds and bats. The following extract from the Exeter Council's Residential Design Guide, for example, details the nesting requirements of common swifts, house sparrows and starlings.

→
Green roof
on Devon
Wildlife Trust
headquarters

→
Starling.
With numbers
declining,
starlings need
assistance
with nesting
sites in new
developments.

Species	Action	Notes
Common Swift	Install internal (swift) boxes at soffits/eaves level	• Any suitable buildings. Proximity of existing colony reinforces need for new nest sites • At least 5m above ground level with unimpeded access • A northerly or well-shaded aspect is essential, avoid southerly elevations and the immediate vicinity of windows • Nest sites should be reasonably close as swifts usually nest in colonies • Broadcasting recorded calls through the breeding season will increase likelihood of occupation
House Sparrow	Install internal boxes at soffits/eaves level	• Suitable buildings within close foraging range of open space and green infrastructure • At least 2m above ground level with somewhere to perch in the immediate vicinity • Needs to be shaded. Easterly aspect is best, avoid southerly elevations • Sparrows prefer nesting in loose groups (10–20 pairs) and boxes can be adjacent to each other, ideally in groups of six or more
Starling	Install internal boxes at soffits/eaves level	• Suitable buildings within close foraging range of open space and green infrastructure • At least 3m above ground level with somewhere to perch in the immediate vicinity • Ideally install a group of nests ideally >1.5m apart • Starlings can be noisy, so their nests are best situated where they will not be a nuisance.[107]

Sustainable drainage schemes

Sustainable Drainage Systems (SuDS) reduce harmful impacts of traditional drainage systems by moderating flows and filtering run-off, allowing natural processes to break down pollutants. They are designed with three objectives in mind:

- to control the quantity and rate of run-off from a development;
- to improve the quality of the run-off; and
- to enhance the nature conservation, landscape and amenity value of the site and its surroundings.

A combination of measures can be used in SuDS including green roofs, permeable paving, purpose-built ponds and wetlands, swales and permeable basins, infiltration trenches and filter drains. All of these features can also enhance nature conservation value by creating new habitat. Swales and basins can be created as features within the landscaped areas of the site. They provide temporary storage for storm water, reduce peak flows to receiving watercourses and facilitate the filtration of pollutants. Ponds or wetlands can be designed to accommodate considerable variations in water levels during storms, thereby enhancing flood-storage capacity.

←
Nesting requirements of common bird species. Table redrawn from Exeter City Council's *Residential Design Guide*.

→
Natural drainage swale.

As with other key considerations, incorporating SuDS needs to be considered early in the site evaluation and planning process, as well as at the detailed design stage. The arrangements for adoption and future maintenance of the system should be considered during the early stages of design. This is likely to influence the design just as much as technical considerations.

Planning policy guidance in England emphasises the role of SuDS and introduces a general presumption that they will be used wherever appropriate. As such, it would be expected that local planning policies and decisions on planning applications relating to major developments (i.e. developments of 10 dwellings or more or equivalent non-residential or mixed development) should ensure that SuDS for the management of run-off are put in place, unless demonstrated to be inappropriate. Local planning authorities should consult the relevant lead local flood authority on the management of surface water, satisfy themselves that the proposed minimum standards of operation are appropriate and ensure, through the use of planning conditions or planning obligations, that there are clear arrangements in place for ongoing maintenance over the lifetime of the development. The SuDS should be designed to ensure that the maintenance and operational requirements are economically proportionate.[108]

Green infrastructure

Green infrastructure is the name given to networks of green space within and around urban areas and often forming links to open countryside. Green infrastructure is ideally capable of delivering a wide range of environmental and quality of life benefits for local communities. Its importance to nature is that it forms a network linking together all types of green space – parks, open spaces, playing fields, woodlands, street trees, allotments and private gardens – providing corridors along which plants and animals can interact and move between different parts of the network (see Case Study 37).

Green infrastructure assets

- Natural and semi-natural rural and urban green spaces – including woodland and scrub, grassland (for example downland and meadow), heath and moor, wetlands, open and running water, brownfield sites, bare rock habitats (for example cliffs and quarries), coasts, beaches, and community forests.

- Parks and gardens – urban parks, country and regional parks, formal and private gardens, and institutional grounds (for example at schools and hospitals).

- Amenity green space – informal recreation spaces, play areas, outdoor sports facilities, housing greenspaces, domestic gardens, community gardens, roof gardens, village greens, commons, living roofs and walls, hedges, civic spaces, and highway trees and verges.

- Allotments, city farms, orchards, and suburban and rural farmland.

- Cemeteries and churchyards.

- Green corridors – rivers and canals (including their banks), road verges and rail embankments, cycling routes, and rights of way.

- Sites selected for their substantive nature conservation value – Sites of Special Scientific Interest and Local Sites (Local Wildlife Sites and Local Geological Sites).

- Nature Reserves (statutory and non-statutory).

- Green space designations (selected for historic significance, beauty, recreation, wildlife, or tranquillity).

- Archaeological and historic sites.

- Functional green space such as sustainable drainage schemes (SuDS) and flood storage areas.

- Built structures – living roofs and walls, bird and bat boxes, and roost sites within existing and new-build developments.[109]

In England, planning policy guidance indicates that:

> Green infrastructure is important to the delivery of high quality sustainable development, alongside other forms of infrastructure such as transport, energy, waste and water. Green infrastructure provides multiple benefits, notably ecosystem services, at a range of

scales, derived from natural systems and processes, for the individual, for society, the economy, and the environment. To ensure that these benefits are delivered, green infrastructure must be well planned, designed and maintained. Green infrastructure should, therefore, be a key consideration in both local plans and planning decisions where relevant.[110]

→
Wild churchyard
in Cornwall.

A good example of such an approach is found at the new village of Cambourne, where green infrastructure was built into the design of the settlement (see Case Study 38).

Climate is an important factor influencing the behaviour, abundance and distribution of wildlife and the ecology of habitats and ecosystems. As our environment alters with climate change, many species will find it difficult to adapt and may need to migrate to find more favourable habitats. Well-planned networks of green infrastructure linking with ecological networks in the countryside outside towns will make it easier for these sorts of movements to occur. Changes in the behaviour and in the abundance and distribution of species are already being observed, with some species declining and others increasing. Some species of birds such as little egrets are becoming much more common in the UK and are migrating further north, whilst others, including some sea birds, are declining due to climate change effects. Over time, these changes are likely to become increasingly pronounced. Maintaining the resilience and capacity of the natural environment to cope with climate change is therefore vital to ensuring a sustainable environment for future generations and to protect and increase species and habitat richness. Providing resilience to change is a key benefit of green infrastructure, underlying the capacity of ecosystems to maintain flows of ecosystem services.

Case Study 38   **Green infrastructure development at Cambourne**

> Cambourne in Cambridgeshire is a new settlement initially developed to provide 4,200 houses. The village has been planned with integrated green infrastructure and new habitat. Existing habitat features were surveyed and used as building blocks for the network of green spaces which permeated three separate 'villages' in the development. Residents have easy access to the whole network of green space which makes up 60% of the settlement. There are 19km of new footpaths, cycleways and bridleways and 16km of new hedgerow. New grasslands are already rich in ground-nesting birds such as skylarks and meadow pipits. The lakes and ponds store rainwater, helping to prevent flooding as well as providing freshwater habitat.
>
> Management of the green spaces is undertaken by the new Cambourne Parish Council, working alongside the Wildlife Trust for Bedfordshire, Cambridgeshire and Northamptonshire. A planning agreement between the Wildlife Trust, the developer and local authorities secured long-term management agreements in return for new office premises for the Trust.

Green infrastructure is the subject of another book in this series of concise planning guides.

Disturbance

Whilst public access and engagement are actively encouraged at most urban nature reserves, more sensitive sites do sometimes suffer from negative impacts of urban or urban fringe locations. For example, disturbance from recreational users and dog walkers, predation of ground-nesting birds by domestic pets and antisocial behaviour – litter, fly-tipping and fire-setting. Concerned about the encroachment of new residential development on sensitive heathland habitats in the Thames Basin Heaths SPAs under the European Habitats Regulations, Natural England researched a zoning scheme to assist in responding to planning applications. Initially it proposed a 5km exclusion zone around all the heathlands. This caused issues for some local authorities – Surrey Heath District Council's entire area was within 5km of a SPA, so any further residential development would have been excluded under such a policy. Following further research, the local authorities whose areas included the Thames Basin Heaths adopted common policies in relation to residential development:

- The establishment of a 400m buffer around the SPA within which no net new residential development will be permitted;
- The provision of Suitable Alternative Natural Greenspace (SANG);
- Strategic Access Management and Monitoring (SAMM) measures and coordinated visitor management across the whole of the publicly accessible SPA.[111]

SANG is a mitigation measure where alternative natural spaces must be provided for recreation and dog walking, for example, to take these pressures off the heaths. This alternative provision is required to be in place before the houses are occupied. Other areas where similar SANG schemes are in place include the Dorset Heathlands (see Case Study 44), Ashdown Forest and the Solent. SAMM is a project to provide management of visitors across the entire SPA and monitoring of the impact. It addresses the issue of cumulative impact of new development across the SPA.

Wildlife organisations which manage nature reserves also sometimes have issues with disturbance from nearby residential areas. Yorkshire Wildlife Trust,[112] for example, researched impacts of damage and disturbance on its nature reserves, identifying

→
Fly-tipping at
Potteric Carr
Nature Reserve,
Doncaster,
South Yorkshire.

five different issues: litter and fly-tipping; damage and disturbance by dogs and other domestic animals; antisocial behaviour including vandalism, graffiti and barbeques; theft and destruction of wildlife and property; and damage by vehicles. Whilst acknowledging that its reserves are managed for people to reconnect with nature just as much as they are for wildlife, the study nevertheless concluded that disturbance does increase with proximity of development to nature reserves. It suggests that new housing developments should be at least 100m from nature reserves, and ideally more than 500m away. Moreover, where this is not possible, the establishment of an ecological buffer, or 'eco-zone', between housing developments and nature reserves could help to reduce the likelihood of antisocial incidents, littering and dog fouling on reserves. Ideally, the 'eco-zone' should be provided within the development site boundary, with its establishment and management funded by the housing developer with ample space designated for various recreational activities.

Most studies of disturbance of sensitive wildlife habitats agree that two-pronged approaches are needed – providing an exclusion zone or buffer around the site to prevent encroachment and alternative natural green space to allow alternative opportunities for recreational activities.

Conclusions

In a rapidly urbanising world, towns and cities have become vital components of ecosystems in the twenty-first century – modern cities need nature just as nature needs cities. The ecosystem services that nature provides – such as adaptation to climate change, increased resilience to drought, flooding and high temperatures, and social health and happiness – are essential to the future of cities. For their part, cities provide refuges for many species of plants and animals becoming scarce elsewhere and, providing they are sensitively planned and the green and blue infrastructure which provide for the habitat needs of those species sensitively managed, wildlife can thrive in cities. Natural green spaces and water bodies, with properly planned natural management of wastes and flooding, should be mutually beneficial for both urban communities and wildlife.

Introduction

Having reviewed the evolution of natural environment policy
and emerging approaches towards planning for the natural
environment, this chapter explores the more operational aspects
of planning for nature, examining the principal planning tools and
policy devices that can help to protect and enhance biodiversity.
More particularly, it explores how the natural environment is
dealt with in national, regional and local plans, development
management, environmental assessment, BAPs, master plans
and design guides.

National, regional and local plans

First, this chapter explores how planning documents at different
spatial scales deal with the natural environment and identifies
some policies which appear to address aspects of the biodiversity
agenda better than others. In the UK, planning is a devolved
responsibility, so there are different approaches in the four
administrations (England, Northern Ireland, Scotland and Wales).

At a national scale, National Planning Frameworks have been
adopted in England and Scotland, and at the time of writing
(2018) a framework was being prepared for Wales. In Northern
Ireland the Regional Development Strategy fulfils a similar role.
These four documents give a policy context for planning for the
natural environment in the UK planning administrations. The
planning frameworks for England and Scotland both promote a
landscape-scale or ecosystem approach towards the natural
environment and encourage the establishment of ecological

networks. In England, after intensive lobbying by the environmental sector following publication of the initial draft framework, the NPPF provides comprehensive high-level policy advice on the natural environment (see Case Study 39).

Case Study 39 **National Planning Policy Framework —**
advice on the natural environment

To protect and enhance biodiversity and geodiversity, plans should:

- plan for biodiversity at a landscape scale across local authority boundaries;

- identify and map components of local wildlife-rich habitats, including the hierarchy of designated sites of importance for biodiversity; wildlife corridors and stepping stones that connect them; and areas identified by local partnerships for habitat restoration or creation;

- promote the conservation, restoration and re-creation of priority habitats, ecological networks and the protection and recovery of priority species populations, linked to national and local targets, and identify suitable indicators for monitoring biodiversity in the plan;

- aim to prevent harm to geological conservation interests;

- where Nature Improvement Areas are identified in local plans, consider specifying the types of development that may be appropriate in these Areas.[113]

Scotland's latest National Planning Framework 3 (NPF3) also addresses the natural environment holistically and includes a 2020 Challenge for Biodiversity that sets out the challenge:

to develop a national ecological network over time
. . . [including] . . . an opportunity to link this with green networks in and around our towns and cities. Benefits will be achieved by taking a long-term, strategic approach to environmental management and enhancement. A landscape-scale approach to environmental planning and management should address the decline in some ecosystem services by prioritising action across river catchments, as well as in and around our towns and cities. This can play a

long-term role in sustaining diversity and delivering multiple benefits, not only for wildlife but also by providing sustainable food, fibre and fuel.[114]

As well as generic policies, NPF3 contains a spatial strategy, with separate strategies for the cities and other regions. The Central Scotland Green Network is shown as a priority for action. However, there is no spatial component in the English NPPF, which only contains generic policies, leaving interpretation to individual local planning authorities in development plans. It is only by examining local development plans that a spatial application of England's NPPF policy is revealed.

Additionally, since regionalism fell out of favour with the change of government in 2010, there is no longer a system of regional planning in England, which is unfortunate as planning policy for nature at the landscape scale is incapable of being addressed satisfactorily within the confines of most local authority boundaries. There is a requirement to cooperate between local planning authorities, but the main driver of this is to tackle housing need; cooperation rarely extends to identifying ecological networks. Whilst there is planning at the city regional scale in Scotland – city regions prepare Strategic Development Plans – and some combined authorities in England are preparing spatial strategies, coverage is piecemeal. In the absence of comprehensive regional planning, a few one-off strategies have been prepared in both countries that address the natural environment at a greater than local scale. Examples include the Green Infrastructure Framework for North East Wales, Cheshire and the Wirral, which also spans the border between England and Wales. A partnership of six local authorities and English and Welsh government agencies, the framework provides a context for coordinating green infrastructure and enhancement of the natural environment which then feeds into local development plans. It proposes seven integrated Environmental Management Areas, broad landscape or river catchment focused zones, intended to deliver a step change in landscape-scale biodiversity enhancement and ecological networks as well as a richer and healthier landscape and a quality setting for towns and villages.

In Scotland, the Central Scotland Green Network provides an integrated approach to planning and environmental enhancement in the central belt, which covers just under 10,000km², with 3.5 million residents, stretching from Girvan in the south-west to Leven and Dunbar in the east and includes the major city regions of Glasgow and Edinburgh. The Network is formed from a partnership of local authorities, government agencies and charities. It applies an ecosystem services approach and aims to achieve large-scale habitat creation around Falkirk and Alloa in particular. Funding has been made available through the lead project partners of the Forestry Commission Scotland and Scottish Natural Heritage.[115]

Local plans form the cornerstone of planning policy in all UK administrations, providing the context for planning decisions affecting the natural environment. In England, local planning authorities are required by the NPPF in their plans to 'take a strategic approach to maintaining and strengthening networks of habitats and green infrastructure; and plan for the enhancement of natural capital at a catchment or landscape scale across local authority boundaries'.[116]

There are many examples where such approaches have been developed in practice, though a recent research project found considerable variability between local authorities (see Case Study 40).

Case Study 40 **Variability of approaches to biodiversity in local plan**

- 'Less than one third of core strategies were found to present a clear strategic approach to planning for biodiversity where the distribution of development is positively influenced by biodiversity considerations and there is coherent planning at the landscape scale'[117]

- On mapping biodiversity assets, the research found that 'where they occur in an authority's area, internationally and nationally designated sites were illustrated in almost 90% plans'[118]

- 'Locally designated sites are not usually illustrated within core strategies . . . priority habitats were mapped in less than 5% of plans . . . [and] less than 20% of core strategies had spatially expressed habitat restoration priorities'[119]

- On ecological networks, 'only 20% of core strategies identify cross-boundary biodiversity that might need to be addressed in cooperation with other local planning authorities . . . [whereas] around 75% of plans include general policy or strategic statements in relation to wider biodiversity enhancement and habitat connectivity, de-fragmentation of wildlife corridors, achieving LBAP [local biodiversity action plan] objectives and securing net gain in biodiversity in the plan period'[120]
- Considering priority species and habitats, 'around 65% of core strategies set a positive or partly positive context for the preservation, restoration or re-creation of priority habitats and the protection and recovery of priority species populations'[121]
- 'Over 75% of plans set some degree of positive context for the conservation and enhancement of species populations outside designated sites. However, these were set as strategic level aspirations'[122]

Overall, this research suggests that local plans have some way to go before they fully reflect even the policies in the English NPPF, nevermind going beyond what is required in national guidance. The issues that appear to be most comprehensively dealt with are policies on internationally and nationally designated sites and priority species and habitats which are also protected by environmental legislation. Protecting local sites (sites identified by local experts, but which are not protected by law), landscape-scale conservation and connectivity are generally more poorly addressed. Nevertheless, there are examples of good practice identified in the report, such as the Ryedale Local Plan Strategy in North Yorkshire which, in addition to addressing many aspects of the biodiversity agenda and unusually for local plans, lists a series of targeted landscape-scale and connectivity priorities to be achieved through the planning process (see Case Study 41).

Excerpt from Ryedale Local Plan Strategy

SP14 Biodiversity. Biodiversity in Ryedale will be conserved, restored, and enhanced by:

- Co-ordinated and targeted activity by public, private, voluntary, and charitable organisations to support the implementation of the Yorkshire and Humber Biodiversity Strategy and Delivery Plan; the Ryedale Biodiversity Action Plan and the Howardian Hills Area of Outstanding Natural Beauty Management Plan

- Providing support and advice to landowners to encourage land management practices that support the objectives, priorities and targets of these plans and strategies

- Minimising the fragmentation of habitats and maximising opportunities for the restoration and enhancement of habitats and improving connectivity between habitats through the management of development and by working in partnership with landowners and land managers

- Maintaining, creating, and improving ecological networks and Green Infrastructure routes to assist the resilience of habitats and species in the face of climate change

- Supporting, in principle, proposals for development that aim to conserve or enhance biodiversity and geodiversity through the prevention of loss of habitat or species and the incorporation of beneficial biodiversity features

- Requiring a net gain in biodiversity to be provided as part of new development schemes

- Resisting development proposals that would result in significant loss or harm to biodiversity in Ryedale

- Encouraging the use of native and locally characteristic species in landscaping schemes

- Investment in the conservation, restoration, and enhancement of biodiversity in Ryedale will be targeted at

The landscape-scale projects identified in the Yorkshire and Humber Biodiversity Delivery Plan which are wholly or partially within Ryedale:

   — Howardian Hills Area of Outstanding Natural Beauty and Western North York Moors Belt

- North York Moors Grassland Fringe
- Vale of Pickering
- West Wolds
- Lower Derwent Valley
- Yorkshire Peatlands

The habitats and species identified in the Ryedale Biodiversity Action Plan including those habitats which are particularly distinctive in the following areas:

- Ancient woodland in the Howardian Hills
- Species rich grassland, a traditional feature of strip fields around Ryedale's villages
- Marsh wetland in the Vale of Pickering
- Fen meadows in the Howardian Hills
- Floodplain swamps in the Derwent Floodplain and streamside swamps in the Howardian Hills and Wolds
- Chalk grassland on the Wolds
- Acid grassland at the foot of the Wolds; southern edge of the Vale of Pickering and Howardian Hills
- Limestone grassland in the Howardian Hills
- Ponds in the Vale of Pickering and at Flaxton
- Dry wooded valleys along the Fringe of the Moors
- Wet woodland in the Vales of Pickering and York; the Howardian Hills
- Wood pasture and Parkland associated with large country houses
- Heathland remnants in the Howardian Hills and southern Ryedale.[123]

—

Managing development

It is equally important that local planning authorities and developers adopt a positive approach to conserving, restoring and enhancing biodiversity through the processes of development. National policy for England identifies a range of biodiversity principles which should be addressed by local planning authorities when determining planning applications (see Case Study 42).

Case Study 42   **Biodiversity principles**

When determining planning applications, local planning authorities should aim to conserve and enhance biodiversity by applying the following principles:

- If significant harm resulting from a development cannot be avoided (through locating on an alternative site with less harmful impacts), adequately mitigated, or, as a last resort, compensated for, then planning permission should be refused;

- Development on land within or outside a Site of Special Scientific Interest, and which is likely to have an adverse effect on it (either individually or in combination with other developments), should not normally be permitted. The only exception is where the benefits of the development clearly outweigh both its likely impact on the features of the site that make it of special scientific interest, and any broader impacts on the national network of Sites of Special Scientific Interest;

- Development whose primary objective is to conserve or enhance biodiversity should be supported;

- Opportunities to incorporate biodiversity improvements in and around developments should be encouraged;

- Development resulting in the loss or deterioration of irreplaceable habitats (such as ancient woodland) should be refused, unless there are wholly exceptional reasons and a suitable mitigation strategy exists. Where development would involve the loss of individual aged or veteran trees that lie outside ancient woodland, it should be refused unless the need for, and benefits of, development in that location would clearly outweigh the loss; and

- The following wildlife sites should be given the same protection as European sites:
    — potential Special Protection Areas and possible Special Areas of Conservation;
    — listed or proposed Ramsar sites;
    — sites identified, or required, as compensatory measures for adverse effects on European sites, potential special Protection Areas, possible Special Areas of Conservation, and listed or proposed Ramsar sites.[124]

British Standard 42020[125] provides a useful code of practice for integrating biodiversity into the planning, design and development process. Addressing information requirements and design, it gives advice on: the pre-application stage; validation and registration of a planning application; the decision-making process; determination and issue of planning permission; and implementation of development. Its guidance is intended for all involved in development projects.

The British Standard describes the overarching aim of planning being to minimise harm and maximise benefits for biodiversity resulting from development. The mitigation hierarchy (see Chapter 2) is identified as a useful discipline in preparing and considering a planning application. Here the hierarchy sets out that development should avoid impacts, if at all possible, mitigate those that are unavoidable and as a last resort compensate for any losses. The Standard outlines processes for deciding whether development proposals are likely to have significant effects on biodiversity and whether proposed mitigation and compensation measures are capable of being delivered through planning conditions or whether obligations will be needed. It suggests obligations might be required to secure biodiversity measures off-site, financial provisions or biodiversity offsets, for example. Planning obligations can be secured in England and Wales through Section 106 of the Town and Country Planning Act 1990, Section 97 of the Planning Scotland Act and Section 40 of the Planning Northern Ireland Order or through the Community Infrastructure Levy, which sets a standard tariff for developer contributions.

A good example of the approach is set out in Case Study 43 for a project at Bowesfield, Stockton-on-Tees, in the North East of England, which demonstrates securing net gains for biodiversity through a planning agreement; in that case between the developer, the local planning authority and the local Wildlife Trust.

Case Study 43   **Development at Bowesfield**

Located on the banks of the River Tees, Bowesfield, Stockton-on-Tees, was an area of derelict and underused land above the floodplain of the river. The floodplain itself was part of the Teesside Development Corporation Estate but, on its demise, was acquired by the Tees Valley Wildlife Trust. It consisted of rough grassland and standing water attracting a range of wetland birds. An adjoining site, in arable cultivation, was also owned by the Wildlife Trust.

The developer, The Banks Group, sought planning permission for a mixed-use development including housing, employment, business premises and leisure facilities. The development area was entirely on land above the floodplain. The developer negotiated with the Wildlife Trust to address the impact of the development on the adjoining areas and eventually the two bodies entered a Section 106 agreement to enhance the wildlife interest on the Trust's land. From the developer's perspective, this would create a multifunctional green network as a setting for the development. The agreement was signed in 2003 and the works were completed in 2007 – the necessary earth-moving operations were undertaken by the developer who also funded landscaping carried out by the Trust. The scheme was carefully designed to minimise disturbance to the nature reserve. Parts of the site were given easy access with surfaced paths and viewing points, others were created as sanctuary areas covertly protected with scrub planting, ditches and bunds to discourage access.

A sum of money was provided by the developer for future maintenance. Landscaping of the floodplain provided a range of new and enhanced habitats including open water, grazing marsh, reedbeds and wet woodland. A separate agreement with the Government's Environment Agency at Preston Farm adjoining Bowesfield provided additional habitat enhancement as part of works to remove flood banks to alleviate flood risk downstream in Stockton and Middlesbrough. The Bowesfield Nature Reserve extends to 53ha of land.

↓
Bowesfield Nature Reserve, Stockton-on-Tees.

> Despite its urban character and location, otters use the
> enhanced wetland habitat which also supports large numbers
> of wetland birds including teal, widgeon, golden plover, curlew,
> lapwing and redshank. Bowesfield is a good example of a
> win-win-win multifunctional development which supports the
> local economy, provides much needed housing and enhances
> the wildlife interest in part of the River Tees Valley.

A rather different approach to mitigating for the impact of
development on wildlife has been used where development has a
general impact on large areas of designated semi-natural habitat.
The approach – the development of SANGs – was first developed
in relation to the proposed redevelopment of Queen Elizabeth
Barracks near Church Crookham, Hampshire. Here, a developer
and the local Wildlife Trust sought to mitigate the impact on
nearby heathland (designated as SPAs) by including within the
development an 'alternative green space' to allow recreation
(especially dog walking) for new residents. Planning permission
was eventually refused (resurfacing a decade later) but the idea
was then taken up by Natural England to resolve the issue of
development in and around the Thames Basin Heaths (see
Chapter 5). In this policy suggestion, developers could mitigate
for development by providing for (or contributing a financial
sum for the local authority to provide) SANGs. The approach
was adopted initially as supplementary planning guidance and
more recently in revised local plans. The approach has since been
extended to the Dorset Heaths – set out in the *Dorset Heathland
Planning Framework*[126] (Case Study 44) – and to the Solent
authorities where development could affect the Solent SAC.

Case Study 44   **Frome Valley Road SANG**

The Frome Valley Road SANG is a 6ha site associated with a
development of 85 houses at Crossways, east of Dorchester,
Dorset. It is currently arable land with low wildlife value.
Planned habitats include grasslands, trees and wetland
features. Crossways is an area planned for housing growth but
lies within 5km of internationally protected heathlands. In
particular the heathland most likely to be used by Crossways
residents is Winfrith and Tadnoll Heath, a Dorset Wildlife Trust
(DWT) reserve which is already subject to pressures from public

use. It is a popular dog-walking site. Having an alternative DWT site for off-lead dog walking would be an extremely valuable complement to efforts to manage access to Winfrith and Tadnoll. In addition, the site lies within the Warmwell to Wool Living Landscape area, making it a high priority location for both habitat enhancement and community engagement.

The requirements for the maintenance of the SANG are simply maintaining an attractive open green space for people and dogs. The funding package has been approved in principle by the developers and will cover the minimum costs of managing the SANG, plus an allowance for inflation and contingencies. There are economies of scale with other nearby DWT landholdings in the area. Of note are the:

- Legal arrangement: 61-year lease initially; if/when a further development nearby is approved, this adds a further 19 years to the lease, i.e. 80 years in total;

- Financial arrangement: lump sum to be paid upfront, based on 61 years' costs of management. Further sum to be added if and when the lease increases to 80 years. The funds agreed make some allowance for inflation. If income from investment was 1.5% that would cover current management costs without reducing the sum invested.

- Current stage reached: Section 106 agreement signed, planning application approved, development not started, waiting on draft legal agreement (December 2017).[127]

An attempt was made to provide a more structured approach to achieving net gains for biodiversity through the planning system in England in 2013, when the Government issued its Green Paper on Biodiversity Offsetting.[128] Several pilot schemes were established in the preceding year, but then enthusiasm appeared to wane and to date there has been no further movement on introducing a formal scheme, though some local authorities have included the approach in local plans (e.g. Warwickshire via the Green Infrastructure Strategy). Biodiversity offsetting does take place though in the Scottish Borders and in many other countries (see Chapter 2). Some local planning authorities have also adopted policies which promote biodiversity offsetting. Somerset County Council published its Biodiversity Offsetting Strategy and Methodology, adopting 'a species-led approach . . . to ensure the maintenance of species' populations affected by development and hence "no net loss" of biodiversity'.[129] Without statutory backing though these schemes require voluntary support from developers which is not always forthcoming.

Biodiversity checklists are a technique used by some local authorities to ensure biodiversity interests are addressed in dealing with planning applications. Aylesbury District Council in Buckinghamshire, for example, screens planning applications against a checklist which identifies features where protected species are most likely to be present (see Case Study 45).[130] This process highlights those applications which require further investigation to ensure any damaging impacts on protected species are avoided. The list includes features such as loft extensions which might otherwise be considered routine, apart from the possibility of protected species, such as roosting bats. Applications requiring further investigation are passed to the council's Green Spaces Team who consider what additional information will be required, including measures to avoid detrimental impacts and mitigate or compensate for them if necessary. This process saves time and effort for both the developer and council staff and ensures planning decisions are taken with the appropriate biodiversity information.

Case Study 45   **Aylesbury District Council biodiversity checklist**

Planning applications which might require further investigation:

- Barn conversions
- Change of use with associated works involving internal alterations to the roof structure
- Hedgerow removal
- Works within 10 metres of a watercourse or 250 metres from a pond
- Works to bridges, underground structures and tunnels
- Works on a designated wildlife site
- Applications which involve demolition
- New build on greenfield and brownfield sites
- Loft conversions [131]

A widely recognised issue with planning conditions and obligations is the difficulty in ensuring that they meet their intended objectives – enforcement over the timescales required to establish new habitats, often many years, has often proved difficult. For example, it takes decades to create new woodlands and many more years, perhaps centuries, for them to mature, which must be addressed in calculating compensation. Provision also needs to be made for long-term maintenance.

→
Brown
long-eared bat.
Biodiversity
checklists
help in the
conservation of
bat species.

Environmental assessment

European and national regulations require that environmental assessment is carried out for certain plans, policies and development projects.[132] Three key assessment processes associated with planning decisions are: SEA, a process to assess the impact of plans and strategies on the environment; EIA of development projects and proposals; and Appropriate Assessment under the Habitats Regulations (HRA). Appropriate Assessment addresses the impacts of plans, strategies and development proposals on European Natura Network sites – SPAs under the Birds Directive, SAC under the Habitats Directive and wetland sites identified under the Ramsar international convention. In England, SEAs of local plans must be prepared as part of a sustainability appraisal which also assesses economic and social effects.

The process to be followed for SEA is specified in regulations and includes: screening to assess likely significant effects on the environment; scoping of the extent of these effects; establishing baseline information against which effects will be measured; preparation of an environmental report which also considers alternatives; consultation; following adoption of the plan preparation of a statement saying how the results of the assessment were taken into account and proposed mitigation; and arrangements for monitoring.

Guidance on incorporating biodiversity into SEA issued by the conservation agencies of England and Wales and the RSPB suggests that it is particularly suited to protecting and enhancing biodiversity because it can:

- build biodiversity objectives into plan development;
- provide an opportunity for those with an interest in, and responsibility for, biodiversity to influence plan-development;
- identify biodiversity-friendly alternatives;
- focus on the longer term and larger scales;
- consider all the threats affecting biodiversity in an area, enabling identification and assessment of cumulative threats and impacts;
- suggest effective mitigation strategies to ensure no net loss of biodiversity throughout the development and implementation of plans, allowing sufficient 'lead-time' to ensure that effective mitigation can be put in place;
- establish monitoring to provide necessary biodiversity data and to enable remedial measures to be taken.[133]

A review undertaken by the European Commission identified a range of issues with SEA, including a view that many assessments were essentially negative, directed more towards mitigating harmful effects than improving the plan by enhancing positive effects. Ideally the assessment should focus on achieving net gains for biodiversity.

EIA follows a similar though much more detailed process that is usually provided by the developer in the form of an environmental statement. Since the regulations were amended in 2017, assessments no longer need to consider alternatives.

Critics of EIAs suggest that they largely react to development proposals rather than influencing their design and often focus primarily on direct impacts rather than indirect or secondary effects and cumulative impacts. A development might have limited environmental effects directly, but these might become significant when combined cumulatively with the effects of other decisions affecting the same or nearby areas or the same animal and plant species.

Where a plan or development proposal might have direct or indirect impacts on a designated or proposed European nature conservation site, it must be subject to appropriate assessment under the Habitats Directive. This entails a screening exercise to identify any likely significant effects and an assessment of those effects on the integrity of the site.

The conservation of one European protected species, the great crested newt, has been particularly controversial in the UK, generating a good deal of criticism from the development industry and elements of the media. Licensing requirements, which involved often extensive surveys and translocation programmes, gave both the species and European Commission nature conservation regulations a bad name, because of the extra costs and delays caused to development projects. This was in a period when the priority in national planning policy was to achieve a step-change increase in rates of housebuilding. The licensing system had also caused frustration for conservationists, as action was focused on newt fencing and often ineffective translocation, rather than on positive habitat management and creation. Such measures had failed to prevent the wider decline of the species and there were concerns about the bad reputation arising for species protection more generally. These criticisms resulted in Natural England reviewing licensing arrangements for protected species generally, stimulating headlines in the media such as 'Great Crested Newts will no longer block housing'.[134] After consulting with stakeholders, greater flexibility will be introduced in licensing, including the option of alternative provision instead of trapping and translocation. This will save time and costs for developers, but it might also help newt conservation by enabling larger areas of suitable habitat to be created away from

→
Great crested
newt.

development sites. There are many issues though in the roll-out
of this policy, with the onus on local authorities to deliver the new
licensing system.

Biodiversity Action Plans

Although not normally viewed as planning documents,
Biodiversity Action Plans (BAPs) and strategies provide valuable
evidence and data on priority species and habitats for use in
preparing development plans and making decisions on planning
applications. In Europe and at the national level in the UK, BAPs
have been replaced by biodiversity strategies (individual country
strategies in the UK).

In Europe, the objective of the biodiversity strategy is to
'halt the loss of biodiversity and ecosystem services by 2020, to
restore ecosystems in so far as is feasible, and to step up the EU
contribution to averting global biodiversity loss'.[135] The mid-term
review assessing progress under the biodiversity strategy,
however, concluded that progress towards meeting this objective
was slow, and

> that the 2020 biodiversity targets can only be reached
> if implementation and enforcement efforts become
> considerably bolder and more ambitious. At the current
> rate of implementation, biodiversity loss and the

degradation of ecosystem services will continue throughout the EU and globally, with significant implications for the capacity of biodiversity to meet human needs in the future.[136]

The UK BAP was replaced by four country biodiversity strategies in 2010. Important actions in the England Strategy were:

- Funding a competition to support the creation of Nature Improvement Areas, in twelve initial areas, providing £7.5 million in the period 2011 to 2015. Lessons learnt will allow us to extend this approach;
- Increasing the proportion of Sites of Special Scientific Interest (SSSIs) in favourable condition;
- Establishing a wellmanaged, ecologically coherent network of Marine Protected Areas (MPAs). By the end of 2016 this will contain in excess of 25% of English waters;
- Agreeing a programme of targeted action with partners for the recovery of priority species.[137]

Online lists provide details of priority species and habitats. Since the strategy was published, the pilot NIAs have been established, but some are still trying to find their niche.

Local BAP translate national and international species and habitat targets to local conditions. In Staffordshire, for example, each local authority has a Local Area Agreement target for BAP habitat creation.

Master plans

Master plans are essentially blueprints for the layout of large-scale new developments. They provide an opportunity to address the natural environment at an early stage in the development process. Town and Countryside Planning Association and The Wildlife Trusts suggest that masterplans should characterise the local habitats and key fauna and flora populations, and should include provision for additional areas of habitat, which reflect locally agreed spatial habitat targets and contribute to national and local biodiversity targets. The master-planning process should also increase biodiversity generally. Masterplans should identify:

- the existing key habitat areas to be protected, restored, enhanced, and expanded;
- transitional and supplementary habitats as part of the wider green space resource, sustaining more widespread habitats and species;
- measures for maximising the contribution of the built and historic environment to biodiversity; and
- existing access and rights of way provisions that are to be protected, enhanced, and expanded without compromising the preceding measures.[138]

The new settlement being built at Cambourne in Cambridgeshire, for example (see Case Study 38), uses a master plan and development briefs to ensure natural green infrastructure is woven throughout the development, giving residents and wildlife easy access to the whole network.

—

Design guides

Design guides are a useful means by which local authorities can highlight the need to safeguard and enhance the natural environment in development projects and illustrate how features such as nesting opportunities for birds and bats can be incorporated into housing designs. They have also been used to encourage natural management of communal areas and green spaces. There are many resources to help planners and developers enhance biodiversity. Organisations such as Town and Country Planning Association (TCPA), Royal Institute of British Architects (RIBA) and Green Building Council have all published guides on the theme of designing for biodiversity. Exeter City Council, for example, provides design guidance to developers aimed at enhancing biodiversity (see page 100). Many other local authorities have produced design guides, often as supplementary planning documents to their development plans, including

The Broads Authority, which has a series of planning guides for biodiversity enhancement for different habitats (meadows, ponds and hedgerows, for example) and species (birds, bats, insects, amphibians, reptiles and fungi).

—

Conclusions

Whilst the tools and policy devices available to planners appear generally to provide adequate guidance on how to protect and enhance biodiversity, the way this guidance is used often falls short of securing positive outcomes for nature. Net gain for nature requires a complex series of considerations including issues such as the distinctiveness and scarcity of particular species and habitats, the time it will take to replace habitats with something of equal or greater value and whether the habitat can actually be replaced. Undoubtedly, better use could also be made of national guidelines in preparing development plan policies on biodiversity and of checklists and codes of practice in managing development. An issue raised by many environmental interests in conversations about planning is also the apparent reluctance of some local authorities to monitor and if necessary enforce planning conditions and obligations.

Introduction

At the beginning of the book we posed six questions about planning for nature:

- Why should planning professionals need to think more about these issues and have a better understanding of how the focus of policy and practice on the natural environment has shifted historically?
- Why do planners need to understand the language of environmental science and what is meant by concepts such as biodiversity, natural capital and ecosystem services?
- Why is it important to plan for the natural environment at a whole landscape scale and to connect fragmented wildlife habitats?
- Why do planners need to look beyond protecting particular species and their habitats, towards rebuilding the whole natural environment?
- Why should planners help nature to recolonise towns and cities and how best can they do this?

Chapters 1 and 2 explained how policy on the natural environment evolved from a weak focus on protecting the rarest species and relatively small areas of pristine habitat through a gradual strengthening in conservation regulation to current policy which is beginning to address whole landscapes and ecosystems. Despite more robust public policy to protect wildlife, biodiversity has continued to decline in the UK and worldwide. Understanding the reasons for these policy shifts helps contextualise current approaches to conserving what remains and restoring something of what has been lost in the natural world. In the UK, the influential report, *Making Space for Nature*,[139] marked a watershed in Government attitudes to the natural environment, consolidated in the years since it was published by policy announcements and increasing public interest in nature. Terms such as biodiversity, natural capital and ecosystem services (Chapter 2) have become increasingly familiar with policymakers and those delivering policy such that they have gradually been incorporated into national planning policy and practice guidance.

Chapter 3 explored why planners need to address biodiversity at a landscape scale and connect habitats together, recognising that one of the principal reasons for the continuing decline of nature is habitat fragmentation. The chapter outlined ecological theory (island biogeography in particular) that underpins these recent policy shifts. Crucially, it is recognised that reconnecting habitats and species, through a combination of larger nature reserves, connecting corridors and stepping stones and more sustainable management of the wider natural environment to create ecological networks is fundamental if we are to address the decline of species diversity and abundance in the UK and elsewhere.

Acknowledging that losses of biodiversity have left the natural environment in a degraded state, Chapter 4 set out how habitats can be maintained, enhanced and, if required, restored and how new habitat can be created. Habitat creation can be remarkably successful. For example, some habitats such as freshwater wetlands are relatively easy to recreate as mobile species of plants and animals colonise them quickly. On the other hand, habitats such as ancient woodland and peatlands are virtually impossible to recreate in meaningful timescales. Notably, the chapter picked up on the concept of rewilding. Here, the aim is not to recreate a fixed objective – a particular habitat or a particular suite of species – but to recreate rich ecological processes, the so-called trophic cascade or a diverse web of life. Rewilding is an unfamiliar approach in the UK though its application is gaining momentum. It is not appropriate where society is keen to maintain those habitats and species that have resulted from the interplay of non-human and human ecology, especially the wildlife of farmed and urban land. These cultural landscapes – such as meadows, hedgerows, heathlands and managed woodlands – are given high value by people and this is reflected in conservation law. It is likely then that a mix of all these different approaches, nested into genuine sustainable development of society, is required to restore the wildlife of Britain.

Chapter 5 explored how, in a rapidly urbanising world, towns and cities have become important ecosystems in their own right. Cities need nature for the ecosystem services that nature provides. These services include adaptation to climate change; increased resilience to drought, flooding and high temperatures; and social health and happiness – all essential to the future of cities. For their part, cities provide refuges for many species of plants and animals becoming scarce elsewhere. Provided urban areas are sensitively planned and managed and include a network of green and blue infrastructure which provide the habitat for species, wildlife can thrive alongside people in urban areas.

Chapter 6 explored some of the mechanisms and policy devices available to planners. It reviewed some of the issues arising in attempts to deliver the new policy agenda and the UK Government and devolved Governments' intents to achieve 'net gains for nature'. Whilst the tools and policy devices available to planners appear generally to provide adequate guidance on how to protect and enhance biodiversity, the way this guidance is used often falls short of securing positive outcomes for nature. Net gain for nature requires a complex series of considerations including issues such as the distinctiveness and scarcity of particular species and habitats; the time it will take to replace habitats with something of equal or greater value; and whether the habitat can actually be replaced. Too often, despite warm words and good intentions, outcomes of development activities over time continue to result in net losses for nature.

Having reviewed the evolution of natural environment policy and the role of planning in delivering it, this chapter looks towards the future and issues which are likely to influence the way forward. One of the key issues here is the UK's exit from the EU (Brexit), as much UK environmental policy is derived from European Directives. Additionally, changes are also emerging to national policy on the natural environment and to planning policy.

The impact of Brexit

There are unresolved issues about how Brexit might influence the future for the natural environment though there are clearly fewer direct implications from the Brexit process in relation to Town and Country Planning, which was never a European competency.

For nature conservation policy, which of course planning regulation must take into account, the decision to leave the EU has more profound implications. European legislation catalysed provisions to finally protect Britain's network of SSSI and, with most environmental legislation emanating from the EU, leaving the Union could dramatically reduce wildlife protection in the UK. In voting to leave the EU, four main issues for the environment arise:

- In principle, the Government has promised to transpose all European law into English and Welsh law through the EU Withdrawal Bill but has yet to set out how the principles behind those laws (for example, the polluter pays principle) and the institutional frameworks used to ensure adherence (for example, the European Court of Justice) will be transposed effectively. The danger of 'zombie' legislation is real. Such issues appear to be understood by DEFRA. In early 2018 (at the time of writing) the Secretary of State for the Environment announced that a new body or bodies to oversee implementation and enforcement of environmental law and principles may be required.
- In addition to the Withdrawal Act, transposed legislation will be amended without full scrutiny by Parliament through the so-called 'Henry VIII' powers. Whilst the Government insists these powers will only be used to

make good legislative gaps, a lack of normal Parliamentary scrutiny could be used to weaken environmental protections yet further.

- Whilst robustly criticised by conservationists for encouraging an intensification of agriculture, coming out of the CAP will end the provisions of the rural development regulation – the so-called Pillar 2 of the CAP. The agri-environment programmes of this policy, though bureaucratic and sometimes poorly targeted, have achieved much. For example, many millions of pounds paid through the CAP by the EU has been used to restore upland blanket bogs in England.

- Likewise, the European Commission also funds a whole range of projects to support its Directives. Of particular importance to conservation has been LIFE and Interreg funding to support large-scale interventions.

That said, EU withdrawal has opportunities. Conservationists have for many years argued for CAP monies to be redirected from income support to farmers (currently focused through the Basic Payment Scheme) to payments for public benefits, such as nature conservation. If payments to land managers remained at CAP levels, but were redirected to public benefits, the impact would be profound.[140]

---

25 Year Environment Plan

The current (2018) Conservative Government set out a manifesto commitment to be the first generation to leave the environment in a better state. This aspiration was translated into strategy through the publishing of a 25 Year Environment Plan. Whilst the objectives of the Plan are applicable to all the UK, policy detail applies only to England. Many in the environmental sector were encouraged by the positive language and the broad range of issues addressed by the plan, which also adopted an ecosystem services approach. For example, it proposed to 'embed an "environmental net gain" principle for development, including housing and infrastructure'.[141] Proposed actions to achieve more positive outcomes for the natural environment through planning and development in the Plan are listed in Case Study 46.

Given that 80% of England's land surface is farmed, strategy in relation to agricultural subsidy is particularly critical. Here, the strategy proposes a shift from income support (the Basic Payment Scheme) to giving farmers and other land managers payments for public goods only. These might include wildlife conservation, natural flood management and soil health and protecting peatlands. Other relevant policy initiatives include support for a Northern Forest; expansion of natural flood management; developing a nature recovery network; connecting people with the environment to improve health and well-being; reducing pollution including from plastic waste; creating more green infrastructure; and introducing a sustainable fisheries policy.

Case Study 46 **Planning and development strategy within the 25 Year Environment Plan**

- Exploring ways in which national spatial data and strategies could support and improve the benefits achieved through environmental net gain.
- Exploring the potential for district protected species licensing to be expanded and include more species, delivering better outcomes for wildlife and a more streamlined process for development.
- Exploring, through ongoing . . . reforms of developer contributions, how tariffs could be used to steer development towards the least environmentally damaging areas and to secure investment in natural capital.
- Determining appropriate locations to pilot a revolving land bank for rural areas.[142]

These are welcome commitments though the paper is rather short on actual policy changes and does not address the issue of resourcing these commitments. Nevertheless, it is a positive start. What now remains to be seen is how these policies are reflected in broader Government policy, including a revised NPPF. Currently (March 2018), a draft review has been published for consultation although the main focus is on new housebuilding rather than better treatment of the natural environment. Nevertheless, it retains key policies on the natural environment (see Case Studies 39 and 42) and strengthens these marginally, referring to the achievement of 'measurable net gains for the environment'.[143]

Concerns have been expressed about the ability of local government and government agencies to deliver many of these ambitious environmental policies after eight years of austerity and staff reductions. Likewise, these commitments may not fully accord with other existing Government priorities, such as the continuing priority for planners to find land on which to build more houses or to build the high-speed railway HS2, which already threatens to destroy irreplaceable habitats such as ancient woodland.

—

Future threats and future actions

Public policy, the right institutions and public funding are of critical importance for Britain to reverse the decline of wildlife. Yet, however ambitious and effective these interventions may be, if framed solely through a nature conservation lens, they may not be able to tackle the more systemic issues of climate change, resource depletion and nitrogen pollution.

A warming climate is already influencing the distribution of animal and plant species, with the rapid northern spread of some species of butterflies and birds, for example. Adapting to these changes will be critical. Serious debate is needed about what sort of ecological communities we should look to conserve. This book details that the UK already needs to move far beyond a system based on protecting particular sites for particular species. Climate change is surely the final nail in the coffin for nature conservation based solely on a site protection and species objectives paradigm, as species assemblages radically change on a rapidly, and likely to be chaotically, warming planet.

Concepts such as 'naturalness' are further complicated by the many thousands of 'introduced' species now found in Britain – those that have escaped from gardens, nurseries, food shipments and fur farms, for example, including some that have been intentionally released into the wild. The conservation movement itself perhaps needs to recognise that it will no longer

←
Speckled wood.
This butterfly
has spread
north as a result
of a warmer
climate.

→
Giant hogweed.
An introduced
species that is
proving difficult
to eradicate.

be possible to manage more than a few very special habitats in ways that maintain historic ecological communities in a human-altered world. In view of the spread of plant diseases, we will perhaps even welcome a species such as sycamore as a natural component of woodlands to replace the elms and ash that are lost to disease. There is also debate about whether we should reintroduce species which were once present but have been become extinct through human activities – reintroducing beavers may now become accepted, but what about the lynx and wolf?

Perhaps in looking towards the future we should look beyond current embedded attitudes towards change and adopt the more optimistic approach promoted by Thomas in 2017, acknowledging that introduced species and new hybrids will eventually form important components of new ecological communities. Thomas sets this out powerfully, arguing that:

> The story of life is one of diversification and renewal – successful genes and species win the game. It is time for the ecological and conservation movement . . . to throw off the shackles of pessimism laden, loss-only view of the world. Why should we not aspire to a world where it is as legitimate to facilitate new gains as avoid losses?[144]

With climate and technological change, the natural world is now in a state of rapid transformation. The challenge for nature

conservation is to develop policy and practice that takes this dynamism into account. As a far more environmentally aware populace moves from education to decision-making institutions and from angry youngsters to voters, public policy needs to catch up. The environment, and how we manage it, is reasserting itself into the centre of British society and politics.

References

1. Sands, T. *Wildlife in Trust – A Hundred Years of Nature Conservation*. The Wildlife Trusts, Newark, 2012.

2. Report of the Wild Life Conservation Special Committee. *Conservation of Nature in England and Wales*. HMSO, London, 1947.

3. Smith, T. *Trustees for Nature. A Memoir*. Lincolnshire Wildlife Trust, Horncastle, 2007.

4. Rothschild, M., and Marren, P. *Rothschild's Reserves – Time and Fragile Nature*. Balaban Publishers, Rehovot, 1997.

5. Lousley, J.E. *Wild Flowers of Chalk and Limestone*. The New Naturalists. Collins, London, 1950, p.78.

6. Nature Conservancy Council. *Guidelines for Selection of Biological SSSIs*. Nature Conservancy Council, Peterborough, 1989.

7. Wildlife and Countryside Link. *The Great SAC Race*. W&CL, London, 1997.

8. Stoneman, R., Bain, C., Locky, D., Mawdsley, N., McLaughlan, M., Kumaran-Prentic, S., Reed, M., and Swales, V. 'Policy drivers for peatland conservation', in Bonn, A., Allott, T., Evans, M., Joosten, H., and Stoneman, R. *Peatland Restoration and Ecosystem Services – Science, Policy and Practice*. Cambridge University Press, Cambridge, 2016, ch.19.

9. http://pubdocs.worldbank.org/en/643781465442350600/Indonesia-forest-fire-notes.pdf.

10. Hayhow, D.B., Burns, F., Eaton, M.A., Al Fulaij, N., August, T.A., Babey, L., Bacon, L., Bingham, C., Boswell, J., Boughey, K.L., Brereton, T., Brookman, E., Brooks, D.R., Bullock, D.J., Burke, O., Collis, M., Corbet, L., Cornish, N., De Massimi, S., Densham, J., Dunn, E., Elliott, S., Gent, T., Godber, J., Hamilton, S., Havery, S., Hawkins, S., Henney, J., Holmes, K., Hutchinson, N., Isaac, N.J.B., Johns, D., Macadam, C.R., Mathews, F., Nicolet, P., Noble, D.G., Outhwaite, C.L., Powney, G.D., Richardson, P., Roy, D.B., Sims, D., Smart, S., Stevenson, K., Stroud, R.A., Walker, K.J., Webb, J.R., Webb, T.J., Wynde, R., and Gregory, R.D. *State of Nature 2016*. The State of Nature Partnership, 2016.

11. Lawton, J.H., Brotherton, P.N.M., Brown, V.K., Elphick, C., Fitter, A.H., Forshaw, J., Haddow, R.W., Hilborne, S., Leafe, R.N., Mace, G.M., Southgate, M.P., Sutherland, W.J., Tew, T.E., Varley, J., and Wynne, G.R. *Making Space for Nature: A Review of England's Wildlife Sites and Ecological Network*. Report to DEFRA, 2010, p.1.

12. The Wildlife Trusts. *A Living Landscape. Play Your Part in Nature's Recovery*. The Wildlife Trusts, Newark, 2010.

13. The RSPB. *Futurescapes: Large-scale Habitat Restoration for Wildlife and People*. RSPB, Sandy, 2001.

14. www.parliament.uk/documents/post/postpn300.pdf.

15. HM Government. *The Natural Choice: Securing the Value of Nature*. The Stationery Office, London, 2011.

16. Humberhead Levels Partnership. *Nature Improvement Area 2012–2015*. Yorkshire Wildlife Trust, York, 2015.

17. www.gov.uk/government/news/letter-from-the-prime-minister-on-cutting-red-tape.

18. HM Government. *A Green Future: Our 25 Year Plan to Improve the Environment*. DEFRA, London, 2018, p.6.

19. Marren, P. 'Where have all the flowers gone? A study of local extinctions as recorded in county floras'. Plantlife. Salisbury, 2000.

20. World Commission on Environment and Development. *Our Common Future*. Oxford University Press, Oxford, 1987, p.43.

21. Department of the Environment. *Sustainable Development, the UK Strategy*. Cm2426. HMSO, London, 1994.

22. Department of the Environment. *Biodiversity, the UK Action Plan*. Cm2428. HMSO, London, 1994.

23. Grigson, W.S. *The Limits of Environmental Capacity*. The Barton Wilmore Partnership, London, 1995, p.24.

24. Jacobs, M. *Making Sense of Environmental Capital*. CPRE, London, 1997, p.42.

25. Land Use Consultants. *Environmental Capacity in Cannock Chase District: Final Report*. London, 2013.

26. ibid., p.97.

27. Jacobs. op.cit.

28. *West Sussex Structure Plan, Third Review: Examination in Public Panel Report*. WSCC, Chichester, 1997, p.10.

29. UNEP, WCMC. *Ecosystems and Human Well-being, a Synthesis*. Island Press, Washington DC, 2005.

30. UNEP, WCMC. *The UK National Ecosystem Assessment.* UNEP, WCMC, Cambridge, 2011.

31. Greater Manchester Combined Authority. *Urban Pioneer Strategic Plan Greater Manchester* (draft). GMCA, Manchester, July 2017.

32. UNEP, WCMC. *The UK National Ecosystem Assessment*, p.7.

33. DEFRA, *An Introductory Guide to Valuing Ecosystem Services*. The Stationery Office, London, 2007.

34. Juniper, T. *What Has Nature Ever Done for Us*? Profile Books, London, 2012.

35. Juniper, T. *What Nature Does for Britain*. Profile Books, London, 2015.

36. ibid., p.253. European Commission. *Nature Based Solutions and Re-naturing Cities: Final Report of the Horizon 2020 Expert Group on Nature Based Solutions and Re-naturing Cities*.

37. European Commission, Brussels, 2015.

38. DEFRA. *Biodiversity Offsetting in England: Green Paper*. The Stationery Office, London, 2013, p.3.

39. OECD. *Biodiversity Offsets, Effective Design and Implementation*. OECD, 2014, p.4. www.oecd.org/env/biodiversity-offsets-workshop.htm.

40. DEFRA. op.cit., p.10.

41. OECD. op.cit., p.3.

42. www.gov.uk/guidance/national-planning-policy-framework/11-conserving-and-enhancing-the-natural-environment, para.109.

43. RSPB. *Planning Naturally: Spatial Planning with Nature in Mind in the UK and Beyond*. RSPB, Sandy, 2013.

44. Cross, A., Sullivan, J., and Colebourne, K. *How the Approach to Biodiversity Offsetting in Victoria Australia is Changing and Potential Relevance to England*. www.epr.uk.com/assets/epr-biodiversity-offsetting-article-inpractice-sept-14.pdf. Accessed 2018.

45. CIRIA, Chartered Institute of Ecology and Environmental Management (CIEEM) and IEMA. *Biodiversity Net Gain: Good Practice Principles for Development*. CIRIA, CIEEM and IEMA, 2016.

46. Town and Country Planning Association and The Wildlife Trusts. *Good Practice Guidance for Biodiversity and Green Infrastructure*. London and Newark, 2012.

47. IUCN, ICMM, *Independent Report on Biodiversity Offsets*. IUCN and ICMM, Gland and London, 2013.

48. MacArthur, R.H., and Wilson, E.O. 'An equilibrium theory of insular zoogeography'. *Evolution*. 17(4), 1963, pp 373–387.

49. MacArthur, R.H., and Wilson, E.O. *The Theory of Island Biogeography*. Princetown University Press, Princetown, 1967.

50. Wilcox, B., and Murphy, D. 'Conservation strategy: the effects of fragmentation on extinction'. *The American Naturalist*. 125(6), 1985, pp 879–887.

51. Kolbert, E. *The Sixth Extinction. An Unnatural History*. Henry Holt & Co., New York, 2014.

52. Waters, C.N., Zalasiewicz, J., Summerhayes, C., Barnosky, A.D., Poirier, C., and Gałuszka, A. 'The Anthropocene is functionally and stratigraphically distinct from the Holocene'. *Science*. 351(6269), 2016, p.137.

53. Lawton et al. op.cit., p.vi.

54. Lovejoy, T.E., and Oren, C.D. 'The minimum critical size of ecosystems', in Burges, R.L., and Sharp, D.N. (eds). *Forest Island Dynamics in Man-dominated Landscapes*. Ecological Studies vol. 41. Springer-Verlag, New York, 1981, pp 7–12.

55. Godwin, Sir H. *History of the British Flora: A Factual Basis for Phytogeography* (2nd edn). Cambridge University Press, Cambridge, 1975.

56. Quoted in Warburton, C. *Green Bridges: A Literature Review*. Natural England Commission Report 181. Natural England, London, 2015, p.12.

57. Catchpole, R. *Planning for Biodiversity – Opportunity Mapping and Habitat Networks in Practice: A Technical Guide*. Research Report 687. English Nature, Peterborough, 2006.

58. Yorkshire Wildlife Trust. *A Living Landscape Yorkshire and Humber. An Ecological Network Approach to Rebuilding Biodiversity for the 21st Century*. Yorkshire Wildlife Trust, York, 2009.

59. Bakker, M., Alam, S., van Dijk, J., Rounsevell, M., Spek, T., and van den Brink, A. 'The feasibility of implementing an ecological network in The Netherlands under conditions of global change'. *Landscape Ecology*. 30(5), 2015, pp 791–804.

References

60. http://ec.europa.eu/ environment/water/water- framework/info/intro_en. htm, Article V.

61. www.catchmentbased approach.org/.

62. The River Torne Catchment Partnership. *The Plan for the Torne Catchment – Our Hardworking River.* Yorkshire Wildlife Trust, York, 2016.

63. www.forestry.gov.uk/ pdf/160329_PBeck_Case Studying_Day_2015_Final. pdf.

64. Holden, J., Green, S.M., Baird, A.J., Grayson, R.P., Dooling, G.P., Chapman, P.J., Evans, C.D., Peacock, M., and Swindles, G. 'The impact of ditch blocking on the hydrological functioning of blanket peatlands'. *Hydrological Processes.* 31, 2009, pp 525–539.

65. Bain, C.G., Bonn, A., Stoneman, R., Chapman, S., Coupar, A., Evans, M., Gearey, B., Howat, M., Joosten, H., Keenleyside, C., Labadz, J., Lindsay, R., Littlewood, N., Lunt, P., Miller, C.J., Moxey, A., Orr, H., Reed, M., Smith, P., Swales, V., Thompson, D.B.A., Thompson, P.S., Van de Noort, R., Wilson, J.D., and Worrall, F. *IUCN UK Commission of Inquiry on Peatlands.* IUCN UK Peatland Programme, Edinburgh, 2011.

66. Natural Capital Committee. *Improving Natural Capital – An Assessment of Progress.* Fourth Report to the Economic Affairs Committee. HM Government, London, 2017, p.2.

67. HM Government. *A Green Future: Our 25 Year Plan to Improve the Environment.* DEFRA, London, 2018.

68. www.wildlifetrusts.org/ sites/default/files/nwa_ summary_document_ digital_final.pdf.

69. Natural Capital Committee. op.cit., p.15.

70. HM Government. op.cit., p.36.

71. ibid., p.32.

72. Lawton et al. op.cit.

73. Godwin, H. 'Pollen analysis and forest history of England and Wales'. *New Phytologist,* 39, 1940, pp 370–400.

74. Brown, T. 'Clearances and clearings: deforestation in Mesolithic/Neolithic Britain'. *Oxford Journal of Archaeology,* 16(2), 1997, pp 133–146.

75. Hoskins, W.G. *The Making of the English Landscape.* Hodder and Stoughton, London, 1955.

76. Rackham, O. *Ancient Woodland, its History, Vegetation and Uses in England.* Edward Arnold, London, 1980.

77. DEFRA. *DEFRA Statistics Cereals Database 1885–2001.* DEFRA, London, 2011.

78. Lindsay, R.A., Charman, D.J., Everingham, F., O'Reilly, R.M., Palmer, M.A., Rowell, T.A., and Stroud, D.A. *The Flow Country. The Peatlands of Caithness and Sutherland.* Nature Conservancy Council, Peterborough, 1988.

79. Pryor, S.N., Curtis, T.A., and Peterkin, G.F. *Restoring Plantations on Ancient Woodland Sites.* The Woodland Trust, Grantham, 2002.

80. Rose, C., Dade, P., and Scott, J. *Qualitative and Quantitative Research into Public Engagement with the Undersea Landscape in England.* Natural England Research Reports, NERR019, 2008.

81. Edwards, J., and Batey, L. *The Way Back to Living Seas.* The Wildlife Trusts, Newark, 2017.

82. JNCC. *UK Biodiversity Habitat Action Plans. Habitat Descriptions. Lowland Meadows.* JNCC, Peterborough, 2008.

83. Webb, N. *Heathlands: A Natural History of Britain's Lowland Heaths.* Collins, London, 1986.

84. Rothschild, M., and Marren, P. op.cit.

85. Davies, A.M. *Nature After Minerals – How Mineral Site Restoration Can Benefit People and Wildlife.* RSPB, Sandy, 2006.

86. Milne, G., and Shennan, I. 'Isostasy: glaciation- induced sea-level change', in Elias, S.A., and Mock, C.J. *Encyclopaedia of Quaternary Science,* vol. 3 (2nd edn). Elsevier, Amsterdam and Boston, 2013, pp 452–459.

87. Field, C.B., Barros, V.R., Dokken, D.J., Mach K.J., Mastrandrea, M.D., Bilir, T.E., Chatterjee, M., Ebi, K.L., Estrada, Y.O., Genova, R.C., Girma, B., Kissel, E.S., Levy, A.N., MacCracken, S., Mastrandrea, P.R., and White, L.L. *Climate Change 2014: Impacts, Adaptation, and Vulnerability. Part A: Global and Sectoral Aspects.* Cambridge University Press, Cambridge, 2014.

88. Möller, I., Kudella, M., Rupprecht, F., Spencer, T.,

Paul, M., van Wesenbeeck, B.K., Wolters, G., Jensen, K., Bouma, T.J., Miranda-Lange, M., and Schimmels, S. 'Wave attenuation over coastal salt marshes under storm surge conditions', *Nature Geoscience*, 7, 2014, pp 727–731.

89. Walker, M.J.C., Coope, G.R., Sheldrick, C., Turney, C.S.M., Lowe, J.J., Blockley, S.P.E., and Harkness, D.D. 'Devensian lateglacial environmental changes in Britain: a multi-proxy environmental record from Llanilid, South Wales, UK'. *Quaternary Science Reviews*, 22(5–7), 2003, pp 475–520.

90. Monbiot, G. *Feral – Rewilding the Land, Sea and Human Life*. Penguin, London, 2014, p.83.

91. Vera, F.W.M. *Grazing Ecology and Forest History*. CABI Publishing, Wallingford, 2000.

92. European Commission. *Nature Based Solutions and Re-naturing Cities.* European Commission, Brussels, 2015.

93. Haase, D. 'Re-naturing the city/Reflections on urban landscapes, ecosystems services and nature-based solutions in cities'. *Planning Theory and Practice*, 2016. http://dx.doi.org/10.1080/14649357.2016.1158907.

94. Scott, M., and Lennon, M. 'Nature-based solutions for the contemporary city'. *Planning Theory and Practice*, 2016. http://dx.doi.org/10.1080/14649357.2016.1158907, p.268.

95. European Commission. op.cit.

96. Haase. op.cit.

97. Land Use Consultants

and SQV Ltd. *Evaluation of the Community Forest Programme: Executive Summary*. London, 2005.

98. ibid., p.4.

99. London Legacy Development Corporation. *Legacy Communities Scheme Biodiversity Action Plan 2014–2019*. LLDC, London, 2013, p.3.

100. ibid., pp 7–8.

101. Marmot, M. *Fair Society Healthy Lives*. The Marmot Review, 2010.

102. DEFRA and University of Oxford. 'Evidence statement on the links between natural environments and human health'. https://beyondgreenspace.files.wordpress.com/2017/03/evidence-statement-on-the-links-between-natural-environments-and-human-health1.pdf.

103. Richardson, M., Cormack, A., Robert, L., and Underhill, R. '30 Days Wild: development and evaluation of a large-scale nature engagement campaign to improve well-being'. *PLOS ONE*. 2016, p.9.

104. Rogerson, M., Barton J., Bragg, R., and Pretty, J. *The Health and Well-being Impacts of Volunteering with The Wildlife Trusts.* Green Exercise, University of Essex, 2017, p.5.

105. Exeter City Council. *Residential Design Guide: Supplementary Planning Document.* Exeter City Council, Exeter, 2010, p.58.

106. The Wildlife Trusts. *Homes for People and Wildlife: How to Build Housing in a Nature Friendly Way*. The Wildlife Trusts, Newark, 2018, p.6.

107. Exeter City Council. op.cit., Appendix 2.

108. Environment Agency, *Sustainable Drainage Schemes (SUDS): A Guide for Developers*. Environment Agency, Bristol, undated.

109. Town and Country Planning Association and The Wildlife Trusts. *Good Practice Guidance for Biodiversity and Green Infrastructure*. London and Newark, 2012, p.4.

110. Ministry of Housing, Communities and Local Government. Planning policy guidance. www.gov.uk/guidance/natural-environment, para.028

111. Surrey Heath Borough Council. *Local Development Framework 2011–2018: Thames Basin Heaths SPA Avoidance Strategy SPD*. SHBC, Camberley, p.10.

112. Rylet, F., Garside, L., and Robin, S. 'Human impacts on nature reserves – the influence of nearby settlements'. *In Practice: Bulletin of the Chartered Institute of Ecology and Environmental Management*, 2017.

113. Ministry of Housing, Communities and Local Government. National Planning Policy Framework. London, 2012 para.117.

114. Scottish Government. *Ambition, Opportunity, Place: Scotland's Third National Planning Framework*. Edinburgh, 2014, p.47.

115. RSPB. *Planning Naturally: Spatial Planning with Nature in Mind in the UK and Beyond*. RSPB, Sandy, 2013.

116. Ministry of Housing. op.cit., para.169.

117. The Planning and Environment Studio. *Nature Positive Local Plans.* RSPB and The Wildlife Trusts, Sandy, 2015, p.5.

118. ibid., p.30.

119. ibid.

120. ibid., p.6.

121. ibid., p.42.

122. ibid.

123. Ryedale District Council. *The Ryedale Plan: Local Plan Strategy.* Ryedale D.C., Malton, 2013, pp 134–137.

124. Ministry of Housing. op.cit., para.118.

125. British Standard Institute. *BS42020, Biodiversity: Code of Practice for Planning and Development.* BSI, London, 2013.

126. Dorset Heathlands Local Authorities. *Dorset Heathlands Planning Framework 2015–2020. Supplementary Planning Document.* Dorset Heathlands Advisory Group, 2016.

127. Case study by Imogen Davenport and Simon Cripps, Dorset Wildlife Trust.

128. DEFRA. *Biodiversity Offsetting in England: Green Paper.* The Stationery Office, London, 2013.

129. Somerset County Council. *Somerset Biodiversity Offsetting Strategy and Methodology.* Taunton, 2013, p.3.

130. Aylesbury Vale District Council. *Biodiversity and the Planning Process.* Aylesbury, 2014. www.aylesburyvaledc. gov.uk/sites/default/files/ page_downloads/ biodiversity-and-the- planning-process-DL- leaflet-NEW_0.pdf.

131. ibid.

132. *The Conservation of Habitats and Species Regulations, SI 2010 490.* The Stationery Office, London, 2010.

133. Countryside Council for Wales, English Nature, Environment Agency, and RSPB. *Strategic Environmental Assessment and Biodiversity: Guidance for practitioners.* 2004, p.15. ww2.rspb.org.uk/Images/ SEAandbiodiversity_tcm9- 257034.pdf.

134. *Daily Telegraph.* 20 September 2015.

135. European Union. EU 2020 Biodiversity Strategy. Publications Office, Luxembourg, 2011, p6.

136. European Community. *The Mid-term Review of the EU Biodiversity Strategy to 2020.* European Community, Brussels, 2015, p.19.

137. DEFRA, *Biodiversity 2020: A Strategy for England's Wildlife and Ecosystem Services.* The Stationery Office, London, 2011, p.5.

138. Town and Country Planning Association and The Wildlife Trusts. op.cit., p.22.

139. Lawton et al. op.cit.

140. Stoneman, R., Whelpdale, P., Gregory, D., and Wilkinson, L. *Applying a New Approach to English Agricultural Policy. Public Payments for Public Goods – an Example of How it Might Work in the River Aire Catchment. A Contribution by Yorkshire Wildlife Trust for a Better Post-Brexit English Agricultural Policy.* Yorkshire Wildlife Trust, York, 2017.

141. HM Government. *A Green Future: Our 25 Year Plan to Improve the Environment.* The Stationery Office, London, 2018, p.32.

142. ibid., p.34.

143. Ministry of Housing, Communities and Local Government. *Draft Revised National Planning Policy Framework: Draft Text for Consultation.* The Stationery Office, London, March 2018, para.173.

144. Thomas, C.D. *Inheritors of the Earth. How Nature is Thriving in an Age of Extinction.* Allen Lane, London, 2017, p.9.